Effective Financial Management

Effective Financial Management

The Cornerstone for Success

Geoff Turner

Effective Financial Management: The Cornerstone for Success

First published in 2011 by
Business Expert Press, LLC
222 East 46th Street, New York, NY 10017
www.businessexpertpress.com

ISBN-13: 978-160649-233-8 (paperback)

ISBN-13: 978-160649-234-5 (e-book)

DOI 10.4128/9781606492345

A publication in the Business Expert Press Financial Accounting collection

Collection ISSN: 2152-7113 (print)
Collection ISSN: 2152-7121 (electronic)

Cover design by Jonathan Pennell
Interior design by Scribe Inc.

First edition: April 2011

10 9 8 7 6 5 4 3 2 1

Printed in the United States of America.

Abstract

In a fast-changing world, brimming with social and economic uncertainty, financial information plays a vital role in the life of an organization and does so with two sets of eyes. One set looks back to see what has happened. This is the accounting function, which is simply about the recording of events and the production of the financial reports that satisfy the stewardship responsibility of management. The other set looks forward to determine the most appropriate strategic direction for an organization, guiding managerial actions, motivating behaviors, and creating and supporting the cultural values necessary to achieve an organization's strategic objectives. This book is all about the second set of eyes, which are the lenses of *financial management*, that help organizations plot their ways through an environment filled with opportunities and dangers.

For students and aspiring managers, as well as those who already have management responsibilities, this book provides an insight, through the eyes of the characters of a start-up company, of some of the ideas and models that help to identify the possible strategies capable of maximizing an organization's value, which is the same as making the owners as wealthy as possible, to determine how to finance the organization in the most proper way, to allocate the collected capital in the most effective way, to monitor the implementation of the chosen strategy to see whether it is meeting the planned objectives, and to reasonably decide on the reinvestment and distribution of profits.

Keywords

financial management, planning, objectives, costs, risk management, debt, equity, analysis, working capital, performance reporting, balanced scorecard, benchmarking, value added, valuation, mergers

Contents

Preface

In a fast-changing world, brimming with social and economic uncertainty, financial information plays a vital role in the life of an organization and does so with two sets of eyes. One set looks back to see what has happened. This is the accounting function, which is simply about the recording of events and the production of the financial reports that satisfy the stewardship responsibility of management. The other set looks forward to determine the most appropriate strategic direction for an organization, guiding managerial actions, motivating behavior, and creating and supporting the cultural values necessary to achieve an organization's strategic objectives.

My book is all about the second set of eyes, which are the lenses of *financial management* that help organizations plot their way through an environment filled with opportunities and dangers. These eyes do this by providing the ideas and models that help to identify the possible strategies capable of maximizing an organization's value, which is the same as making the owners as wealthy as possible, to determine how to finance the organization in the most proper way, to allocate the collected capital in the most effective way, to monitor the implementation of the chosen strategy to see whether it is meeting the planned objectives, and to reasonably decide on the reinvestment and distribution of profit.

Thinking along these lines provides an ideal way of structuring the book. There are five key sections, each containing one or more chapters. The sections are as follows:

- Where are we now?
- Where do we want to be?
- How do we get there?
- How do we know that we've arrived?
- Where to next?

Throughout the book I'll be relating financial management to strategy through the use of a case study, which will be used in each chapter to explore that topic. I have chosen a business start-up as the basic building block. The reason for this being that with a start-up, you are working with a clean canvas. There is no history to get in the way of achieving your goals or distorting the perspective. In the same way, there is no strategy or financial management in place, and all the key issues need to be thought through from first principles.

I do hope that you'll engage with the characters I have created and try as hard as you can to visualize the situations they find themselves in. As with any case study there are no perfect answers, just some ideas that might be better than others in any given situation. A quick word of caution: The case study is not meant to be a guide for those wishing to start in business, as I concentrate on a limited number of areas. There are a number of other very important, practical areas that I do not cover at all. After the health warning it is time to introduce you to Pearl.

Case Study

The Concept of Bull-Roo Enterprises Limited

As a baby, Pearl King was "transported" from her war-ravaged and impoverished homeland as her parents sought to establish a new life for themselves and their family in the Great Southern Land. Over the years, Pearl proved herself to be an exceptional student and achieved encouraging results in her studies, both at school and at university. Indeed, she had earned a promising management career with a multinational computer hardware company when she decided it was time to start her own family.

Now more than 30 years later, Pearl is recently widowed. Recognizing that she must provide for herself, Pearl decides to start up her own business as she does not believe reasonable employment will be easy to secure, especially considering her age and the length of time she has been out of the workforce. What, though, to do?

Prior to her husband's death, they, with their children, were avid travelers exploring the world, enjoying everything the diversity of cultures offered, and, more importantly, making lasting friendships in many countries. Maybe there was an opportunity to develop some trading links with some of these old friends? But what to trade? Rather than focus on a specific product, or range of products, Pearl decided to keep her options open and began to contemplate a trading house along the lines of the great Japanese traders of the 1960s and 1970s.

Acknowledgments

For their indirect contribution, I will always be indebted to my students, past, present, and future, in both graduate and undergraduate classes, whose questions, comments, and witticisms contribute to and enhance the content of my courses and the way I communicate the story I have to tell. They were, are, and always will be a source of inspiration to me.

There are special thanks to my son, Keith, who is a superb graphic artist and contributed to the book by taking some of my rough sketches and producing some really good illustrations.

I am also grateful to the team at Business Expert Press, particularly to David Parker for having faith in my ability and giving me the opportunity to produce this book, and to Ken Ferris and Cindy Durand for their support and helpful advice during its creation.

PART I

Where Are We Now?

Our friend Pearl wants to start a trading house. For better or worse, the world is quite a bit different now than it was in the early days of the great Japanese trading houses, the *sogo shosha*—総合商社 literally meaning *all round trading* company—which I'm sure she understands only too well. Perhaps the most significant change to impact her idea is that technology now makes it much easier for buyers to deal directly with suppliers. Is there really a place for a trading house anymore?

Well as the French like to say, *plus ça change plus c'est la même chose*. For suppliers, the cost of dealing with a large number of customers, some of whom only buy in irritatingly small quantities and some of whom can be quite demanding, is something they would like to avoid if they can. Sure, with a good understanding of their cost structures they can charge these smaller customers a higher price for their product or service, but somehow that really never quite matches the additional burden on their business associated with these customers. Having fewer, larger customers is much more manageable and often more profitable in spite of predictably lower selling prices. So yes, perhaps there is a niche for a trading house. Those technological changes that made Pearl question the prospect of her idea may yet prove to be the foundation of her success.

> ***Think!***
> Having doubts? Then think of what Amazon.com has done for book publishers.

With a little more confidence that success is probable, Pearl starts to plan the journey for her business venture. She is thinking of many things that need to be considered, some of which are obvious and others not quite so. Where to start?

Think!
What would you be thinking about? Make a list and compare it with the one that follows.

Let's make a list, not in any particular order, for the moment:

- What do I want to sell?
- Who can I get it from?
- Who could I sell it to?
- What's the best way to structure the organization?
- Who will help me?
- What resources will I need?
- How much money will I need?
- Where will I get the money I need?

That's not a complete list, of course, but it will get her started. The more she thinks about it, the more she realizes that she will not be able to get this venture underway all by herself. Some things Pearl can do. Indeed, the first three items on the list are best handled by her. She needs to decide who of her friends around the world will best be able to help her, whom she feels more comfortable dealing with, and what she can buy from them. Then she needs some market research to help decide on the best products to include in her range. Although not really a financial management issue right now, at some point, and not too far away, there will be a need for some input from a financial management specialist.

The immediate need is for some input from that specialist to decide on a legal form and structure for the organization, and for the last three items on that list. No one in her family has that background, so Pearl needs to move quickly to get access to someone with this expertise as it will be vital to the financial health and overall profitability of her organization. The person she chooses should not be a bean counter, the person who balances the books each month and writes paychecks, but rather a financial planner, who has a good appreciation of the business, continually monitors performance, reports results, and is constantly alert to financial warning signals so that corrective action can be taken in time.

It's important not to have the wrong person in this role, and it's equally important to give that person the opportunity and encouragement to perform this important task.

Pearl has someone in mind, a trusted confidant of her late husband, who she believes will do a superb job. It is time for some fast, sweet-talking so she can get on with realizing her dream.

CHAPTER 1

In the Beginning

Introduction

Shakespeare once wrote, "We are such stuff as dreams are made on,"[1] and so it is with our business organizations. They exist simply as a result of putting dreams into action. Dreamers, by themselves, rarely have all the necessary skills to put their dreams into effect. The doers rarely achieve very much unless their energy is properly focused toward a clearly defined goal. Together they can achieve a great deal.

Translating this to the commercial world, no one part of an organization can deliver everything that is needed. Put it this way: Marketing by itself can do nothing unless it has a product or service to sell, which will be delivered by operational departments. Similarly, the accounting department has nothing to account for unless the business is making, marketing, and selling its products or services. It is this interdependence that pervades this book.

How do you picture interdependence? Well think of a wheel like the organizational one that is shown in Figure 1.1. When a wheel is properly constructed, it will turn smoothly and enable the user to get where they want to go more quickly and easily, and so it is with any organization's wheel. Strategy can be likened to the hub of the wheel, the focus of the forces that will make the wheel turn. Radiating out from the hub are all the spokes that represent each of the different functions within an organization. The rim that helps to keep all of these spokes in place and maintains the integrity of the wheel is the financial management function. If any one element is missing, the wheel will quickly become distorted giving a very bumpy ride indeed before collapsing in a tangled mess!

Figure 1.1. An organizational wheel.

Think!
Picture the wheel of your organization. Is it strong, or is the hub, rim, or one of the spokes weak and creating a problem?

It's easy to see how important it is not only to recognize that there are many different strands to an organization that need to work together but also to understand how they work together to create value.

Deciding the Objectives

In our bicycle wheel, the hub represents an organization's strategy, which is the focal point of everything that it does. Because it draws on, and then contributes to, each of the business disciplines, it is not considered a discipline in its own right. What's more, it probably isn't really a function but more of an agenda: a series of fundamental questions and problems that concern organizations and their successful development. In other words, it's about the future accomplishments of the organization, and so the imperative is to address these questions and problems by whatever means we have at our disposal.

The strategy agenda is concerned with three levels, which are inextricably linked in much the same way as the personal telescope shown in Figure 1.2. We must not only consider the success of the organization when deciding the objectives but also think about the environment in which we operate and the individuals whose actions help shape the organization's accomplishments.

Where does financial management fit in all of this? Well think back to the wheel, and you'll see that the rim represents financial management. As we contemplate and decide on the objectives for each of the business functions, the spokes, we need to understand the financial implications of each objective to ensure that we are eventually going to meet the needs of the owners.

The Organization

As I have already suggested, all of the functions of an organization must operate in concert with each other. We, as owners, must understand the needs of its organizational form; the laws governing its operation; and all of the standards, responsibilities, and obligations involved. This means we need to develop sound practices of communication, as well as monitoring and controlling all activities.

Whether an organization is starting from scratch, like the case study in this book, or is an ongoing business, the needs are the same. The organization must have a basic form—a sole proprietorship, a partnership, a company, or a trust.[2] Which to choose? Each has its own advantages

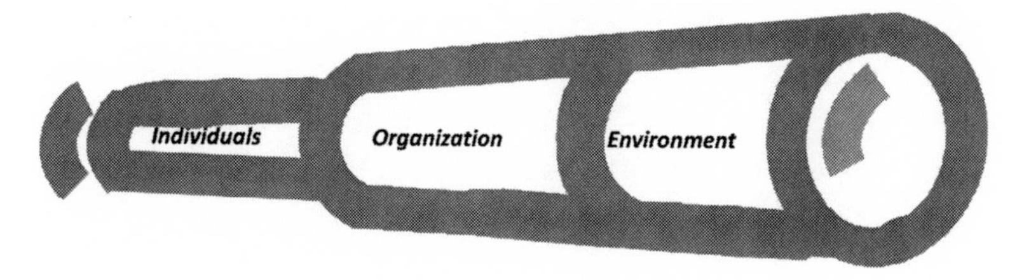

Figure 1.2. The strategy telescope.

and disadvantages in four key areas of consideration—continuity, liability, administrative burden, and contribution to society. The first two organizational forms do not legally separate the organization from its owners, creating problems with continuity and liability. The third and fourth organizational forms overcome those problems but enforce an increased administrative burden. The contribution to society, in the form of taxes, may be different for each of the organizational forms depending on regulations in force at any given time and in any given place but will ultimately depend on the extent of business activity and the level of profit achieved by the organization.

The choice, which may always be changed at a later date, will reflect our personal view as owners. Nevertheless, each form of operation has statutory and practical requirements, some of which are different and some of which are the same. Whichever form is chosen, we need to create a management structure to fulfill these requirements. Generally, our external financial advisor will jog our memory about these needs, but the responsibility to satisfy them lies with us, as does sound management of the organization.

Importantly, in terms of financial management, every business structure considers the same things, which are those that impact the monetary situation. In essence, any business exists to prosper and make money for the owners. This requires a sound business plan, a good understanding of the financial activities that underpin our organization, and effective accounting for the organization's activities. Understanding why each of these things is important will become clearer as you progress through this book.

For those of you who are going solo, questions about how you can implement all of the suggestions contained in this book will arise. Let's be honest. It's just not possible to do everything yourself. What I hope you will do is look at your organization and the way you operate it and compare what you see with the ideas put forward in this book. Then isolate the activities you consider essential. Can you cope with those on your own? If you decide that you can't, then as our friend Pearl is about to do, go and ask a specialist for help. In many cases, the benefits that you get from a specialist's advice will far outweigh the costs.

Money to Start With

All organizations need capital to survive. If you are just starting out, then a good rule is to have between 1 and 2 years of both business and personal expenses covered before embarking on a business venture. All well and good, but how much is it and where does it come from?

> ***Think!***
> If you recently started out in business, or are thinking about it, then where did, or will, your initial investment come from?

In better economic times it might have been possible to negotiate a loan from a bank for some start-up capital, but there would be no way that the bank would have lent us all we need. It's our venture, not theirs, and so they would have expected us to put in the majority of the initial investment required to get the business up and running. Following the global financial crisis, it is almost certain that we shall have to provide all of the initial investment ourselves. We might still be able to get a loan if we are able to offer some security. More importantly, for business loans, lenders now want to see a positive operating and financial track record with all loan applications, and since we are just starting out we don't have that.

So let's break open the piggy bank and put as much as we personally can into the initial investment. If that's not enough, then let's talk to grandparents, parents, siblings, and friends to see if any of them are prepared to help get the venture underway.

Case Study

The Birth of Bull-Roo Enterprises Limited

On page 2 there was a list of some questions that Pearl needed to think about. For this chapter there are three that are pertinent, and we'll try to decide on them now.

What's the Best Way to Structure the Organization?

No longer a young person, Pearl needs to think carefully about how she should structure the organization. The first thing she needs to do is to decide on its legal form, which means she needs to consider the continuity, liability, administrative burden, and contribution to society aspects of organizational form. She considers the last of these the least important, since if the venture is successful then that will take care of itself. Her main worries lie in the continuity of her business and what might happen to her personal financial situation should the venture fail.

Pearl has decided that there really is no alternative other than to structure her venture in the form of a limited liability company. Importantly, this organizational form will protect her personal finances in the event of failure and, by including her children as shareholders, will facilitate continuity of the venture should she no longer be able to take part in its life. Taking this path does have one drawback, however, and that is an increased compliance and administrative burden. Pearl has decided that the benefits of operating as a limited liability company far outweigh the costs, and so that's the way it will be. After a quick phone call to her lawyer, Bull-Roo Enterprises Limited is on the way to being formed.

How Much Money Will I Need?

This is not an easy question to answer. Before Pearl can answer it, she needs the beginnings of a plan. Sure, she has a vision but has not yet devoted the time to translating that vision into a formal plan. What's more, she is sure that she can't do it by herself. She must speak to Keith, her late husband's trusted confidant and longtime family friend, to see if he is prepared to help her. She picks up the phone and invites him for lunch on Sunday—an offer he simply cannot refuse. Pearl is certain he will agree to be part of the team, and so planning the way ahead can wait for a few more days.

Where Will I Get the Money?

OK, Pearl doesn't know quite how much money she will need just yet, but she does know where it will come from. Her late husband's life insurance payout is still sitting on deposit in the bank. She believes that will be sufficient to get started, but she'll know for sure once she and Keith have finished the plan. If she needs more, then she knows enough people in the financial world that she is sure one of them will be able to help.

Summary

In terms of getting our business venture underway, we don't appear to have progressed very far, but that's not important. What is important, as with any structure, is to ensure that the foundations, or supports, are well designed and laid in such a way that the structure remains sound for many years to come.

We've considered the issues associated with organizational form and made our decision about the best shell in which to construct our business venture. We understand the need to develop a good plan that sets out the objectives for each of the business functions and clarifies the financial implications of each objective. We shall look at this task in chapter 2. And we've come to terms with the fact that the initial investment needs to come from our own resources, or those of family and friends, because in the current economic climate lenders aren't too keen on providing loans where there might be anything more than minimum risk.

So let's see what happens after Sunday lunch!

PART II

Where Do We Want to Be?

What happened after Sunday lunch? Well having been plied with a succulent meal, some excellent red wine, and lots of heartfelt compliments, Keith, a qualified accountant and longtime company secretary of a manufacturing company, was persuaded to be part of Pearl's new venture. As someone who was now semiretired, he wasn't looking for an executive's salary and benefits package, preferring to settle for a small salary and a share in the business, for which he would make an agreed-upon cash contribution. For Pearl, that was two birds with one stone; she not only got some useful and reliable support for her venture in areas where she really needed it but also got a contribution to the initial investment. No wonder she was smiling as she waved good-bye to Keith. They had agreed to meet again in the week ahead to get the planning process underway.

Like Pearl, most of us have a vision of what we would like to achieve and where we would like to be at some point in the future. Identifying one or more great ideas that we think will help us along the path toward that vision is something we have to do. That those ideas fit within our overall objectives is a great start, but making sure that we know how to translate them into deserved rewards is the name of the game. Making both long- and short-term plans, understanding exactly what really happens, and evaluating and analyzing performance are all important parts of this translation process.

The ideal planning process does not start from the bottom and work its way up to the top. It begins at the top of the planning tree, as pictured in Figure 2.1, where we have identified our impressive idea(s), and travels downward to the lowest level of the organization. As you will see later, this doesn't mean that we disregard the contribution that those who are subordinate to us can make. It simply means that we start by developing a strategy to achieve our vision and then build operating plans that will provide an effective execution of strategy.

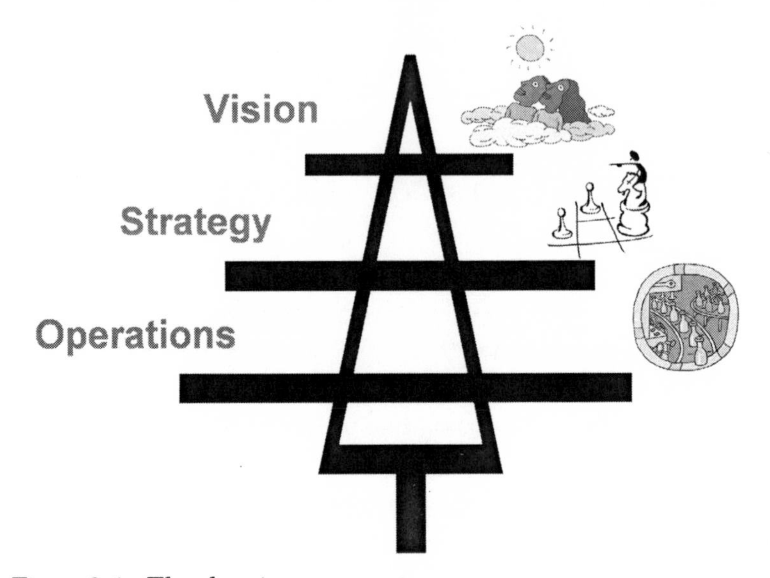

Figure 2.1. The planning tree.

> ***Think!***
> Is this the way you go about planning in your organization? Maybe you do it differently, but does it work?

In the next chapter you will learn about plans and budgets: what they are, how they may be prepared, and how they are used. You will also be introduced to the importance of communication in the process of establishing plans and budgets as well as the human aspects of the process.

CHAPTER 2

Planning to Get There

Introduction

The planning tree identifies three stages in the planning process; but unlike a tree that only grows upward, business planning is a continuous, circular process as depicted in Figure 2.2. Starting with our vision statement, which sets out the objectives of our venture, we then develop the strategic plan that will shape the nature of the business and the type of markets that we plan to operate in. This plan defines our relationships with our competitors in our chosen market environment. Once the strategic plans are in place, we can begin to develop more detailed operational plans to ensure we properly think through what it will take to keep our business in motion. These plans should explain, in simple language, how each functional aspect of the organization—administration,

Figure 2.2. The planning cycle.

finance, marketing, operations, procurement, and sales—will contribute to the effective execution of strategy. A clear articulation of the tactics for each of the functional areas demonstrates clarity of thought and purpose and will be used later to gauge the success or otherwise in meeting our objectives.

The creation of a vision statement is important for just about any type of organization. Essentially, a vision statement takes into account the organization's current status and identifies the direction in which it wishes to go. In other words, it is not about what the organization currently is, but what it hopes to become. By describing the central aim that our organization aspires to, the vision statement helps to provide a focus for our strategy and operational activities.

In essence, the vision statement is intended to be no more than a couple of sentences that clearly outline the specific aim of our organization without providing the details of how that aim will be reached. It allows us to identify a direction for our organization without inhibiting the development of a strategy that will allow us to reach that lofty goal.

Think!
Has your organization articulated its vision? Does it clearly outline the specific aim of the organization?

With the key aim of the organization decided and a vision statement constructed, every organization begins to make plans. As we can see from Figure 2.2, this ought to be a two-step process. First, we need to develop strategic plans. Second, we translate those strategic plans into operational plans. Before we embark on what that entails, we should remember that a plan is a guiding light. It is not something that is done once a year in order to develop a fancy report and then is forgotten. In fact, our plans need to be very live documents undergoing continual change and revision.

For Pearl and her friend Keith, as they struggle to find their company's place in the world and carve out a unique position, it will not be unusual to find large discrepancies between the numbers in their plans and their actual performance. This brings us to the final stage in the planning cycle, the performance measurement stage, which will be explored in part 4 of this book. For now it is enough to understand that we need to know exactly what those discrepancies are. The reasons for the deviations need to be analyzed so that we are in a position to create a revised plan. It is, as I have said before, a continuous process.

Planning

Some plans are more formal than others, and some organizations plan more formally than others, but all make some attempt to consider the risk and opportunities that lie ahead and how to confront them. Planning requires us to lift our gaze from the day-to-day problems, which beset our organization, and to make an attempt to see what the future holds. Planning also allows us to be proactive in managing the business as opposed to being reactive. Waiting for unknown catalysts to initiate and prompt action places our organization at greater risk and at a severe disadvantage to more aware and prepared competitors. Being proactive means being prepared, allowing our organization to develop some resilience to any potentially damaging forces from its external environment. These could be the actions of competitors, government, and unions as well as changes in the economy. In so doing we ought to plan at both the strategic and operational levels. Yet in many organizations, this may not always happen as I ought to make clear.

By implication, strategy involves competing. If you have no opposition, then you do not need a strategy, and hence there is no need to prepare a strategic plan. If only it were that simple. Few, if any, organizations operate in a competition-free environment. Some may think they do, but often that's only because they do not truly understand, or have a blinkered view of, the nature of their business activities. This comes about because they don't understand all the sources of competition. Let me explain with an example. If you think of a short-haul airline, then in what competitive environment does it operate? Most people would immediately think of the highly competitive budget airlines as well as the short-haul operations of the full-service airlines and develop their strategic plans based on that premise. But, and this applies in China, Japan, and Europe in particular, another source of competition is the high-speed rail services, which are considered competitive on journeys up to 4 hours.

For most organizations strategic planning is indispensable. This requires us to decide in what markets we would like to operate, or *domain*

Think!
Are you clear about your organization's competitive environment?

selection, and how we should operate in those markets, or *domain navigation*. In terms of value creation, this translates to asking in what markets should our organization seek to create value, and in what ways should it seek to create value? This may be best achieved by doing the following:

- identifying, developing, and exploiting the strengths, often called core competencies, of our organization that will give us a competitive advantage in the markets in which we choose to operate
- identifying the markets where these core competencies may be best deployed
- covering any shortages in required capabilities by investment in tangible and intangible resources
- applying our organization's available capabilities to the markets where they may be most effectively exploited
- erecting barriers to prevent our competitors from encroaching into our areas of competitive advantage

Given that organizations need to undertake these activities effectively, assistance is required from the financial management discipline to provide the financial backdrop for making the decisions. All the same, our planning team must appreciate that although this input is likely to be significant, there are factors other than the purely financial to reckon with in most decisions. There is something else our planning team needs to understand. Although a sense of direction is important, it can stifle creativity, especially if it is rigidly enforced. Strategic planning will add little value—indeed it may well do harm—if our organization's strategic plans are designed to be used as detailed blueprints for our managers.

Around the middle of the 17th century, Miyamoto Musashi, a samurai warrior, wrote a book titled *五輪書*, which translates to *The Book of Five Rings*, about military strategy, which is widely appreciated by many business leaders who find its discussion of conflict and advantage to be relevant to their work. The story of the second ring, water, is most closely related to strategy. In relation to life, the meaning of *water* is *flexibility*. Water demonstrates this naturally as it changes to fit within the boundaries that contain it, seeking the most efficient and productive path. In the same way our organization should be capable of changing when presented with new information about its competitive environment. In the erratic and confusing times in which we live, fluidity can be more important than a finely tuned strategic compass. Our strategic plan then should be seen as laying out the general path—but not the precise steps—by which our organization intends to create value.

How will Pearl and Keith construct their path? I mentioned earlier that strategic plans should explain, in simple language, how each functional aspect of the organization will contribute to the effective execution of strategy. There is a logical sequence to this, which is reflected in Figure 2.3. After all, we can't really begin to put a procurement plan together unless we know what it is we intend to buy and sell. Marketing and sales must come before procurement. Likewise, we need to know how we plan to operate, and in what environment, before we can start to think about the financial aspects of our plan.

When we've been around the circle once, is that the end? Is it finished, and can we move on? Highly unlikely! What is more likely is that we find the sales and procurement plans don't quite fit together as they

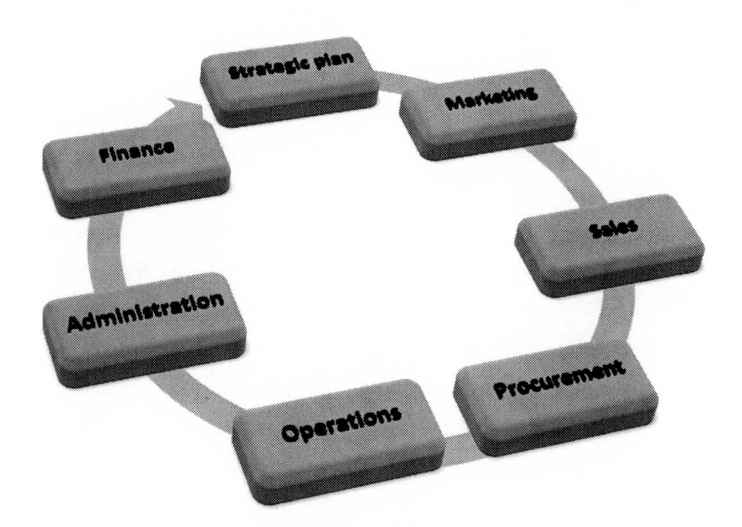

Figure 2.3. Strategic planning sequence.

should or that the financial aspects of our plan are untenable. Unfortunately, we can't just shrug our shoulders and hope that it will all come together either when building the operating plans or, even worse, when we are actually trying to turn our strategic plan into reality. We need to go around again and again and again until we have a version of the plan that will satisfy our vision and that appears to be fully functional.

Think!
Does your organization produce strategic plans? If so, then is the process the same or similar to this?

Once the strategic plan is in place, the task of creating annual operating plans designed ultimately to achieve our organization's strategic objectives can start. This process, more commonly known as budget preparation, tends to fill anyone familiar with it with dread. It is often seen as painful, and it is not always clear whether the effort that is required leads to any productive output. What's more, the validity of the budget document becomes questionable because of the time lag between its preparation and its application. Nevertheless, it is imperative that we carefully plan our organization's affairs to achieve financial success. So perhaps we can avoid using the word *budget* and refer to our completed document as the *annual operating guide*.

Each functional area will consider, in more detail, how they will put the strategic plan into operation and document this in a functional plan. In a number of organizations, either because of the nature of their business or because of the environment in which they operate, they do not plan formally for much longer than the year ahead. Nevertheless, their annual operating guide must be set in the context of strategic plans, which are likely to exist even if they have not been made explicit. In other organizations the opposite is the case with the strategic planning process being terribly formalized. So much so that considerable effort is put into converting the first year of the strategic plan into highly detailed operating plans and subsequently monitoring performance against them.

For our annual operating guide, while much of the work will be done inside each functional area, we can't do it in a completely isolated way. As you can see from Figure 2.4, this collection of plans, which is expressed

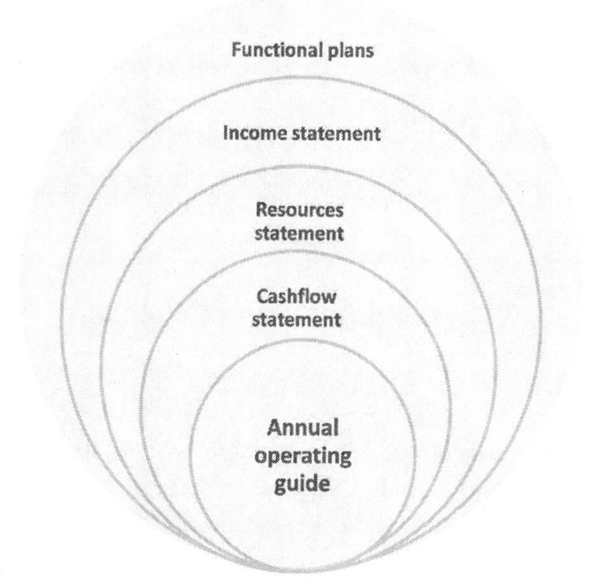

Figure 2.4. Key annual planning documents.

largely but not exclusively in financial terms, is collated to form a document against which actual performance will be measured. This document contains not only the functional plans but also three statements for the organization as a whole. These three documents are the income statement, the resources statement,[1] and the cash-flow statement. Only when these three organization-wide statements are completed will we know if our plan for the coming year is likely to make sense. Preparation of the annual operating guide is a job for the financial management team, and it epitomizes the wheel concept depicted in Figure 1.1 on page 6.

Clearly, then, the most important element in the planning process is management—the individuals and the managerial process. This is evident in the planning framework that has been discussed in this chapter and comprises making our organization's vision explicit, determining the strategy necessary to achieve the vision, creating strategic plans, designing the planning system and its implementation and operation, and designing the monitoring routines and the ultimate rewards and penalties for success or failure. Plans have to be a management tool rather than merely an accounting exercise.

Expectations, as encapsulated in our strategic and operational goals, are thereby clearly proclaimed in our planning document. In the second phase, the goals laid down for each function in our organization will provide the basis for performance evaluation and any corrective action. Throughout our organization, performance will be compared to expectations and rewards or admonishments distributed on the basis of those comparisons.

Behavioral Aspects of Planning

All financial statements and reports are intended to affect the behavior of one or another group of people. Plans are intended to affect the behavior of all the individuals involved in or with our organization to encourage them to work toward our objectives and to do so in a coordinated way. Unfortunately, some individuals may not always behave in the best interests of our organization or they may be unwilling to work hard enough to achieve the goals, or targets, that have been set. This is known as *dysfunctional behavior*. When we set about designing the planning system, we need to do it in such a way that we minimize the occurrence of such behavior. This requires us not only to think about the system's aspects of the planning process but also to consider the human aspects. These are numerous, and many of them are interrelated. The most important are motivation, participation, and communication.

Think!
What human aspects did your organization consider when designing its planning system?

Our planning system will not be successful if individuals do not want to achieve the targets that have been set for their area of responsibility. There are many reasons for such a lack of motivation, but the key ones relate to an individual's aspiration level, which is the level of performance that they have set as a personal target, and a perception that there is inadequate provision for the recognition of achievement.

As far as individuals are concerned, if the performance targets are set too far above their own aspirations, then they may become frustrated or disenchanted and inclined to reject the plan as unrealistic. They will not have any motivation to succeed. Alternatively, they may feel inclined to *cook the books* in an effort to reach unrealistic targets in the expectation that time will make up for their temporary problem. This initial, seemingly harmless, act is often followed by an escalating pattern of deception that may ultimately lead to the collapse of our organization.

On the other hand, if the performance targets are set too far below their aspirations, then an individual may be demotivated by the lack of a challenge and may work at a level of performance below that which could otherwise have been achieved. On the expense side of the equation, this is likely to have the undesirable consequence of encouraging waste.

Failure to recognize and reward achievement is also seen as a demotivating aspect in the planning system. How then should we recognize achievement in the first instance and reward it subsequently? While the immediate reaction is that rewards should be financial, which automatically acknowledge achievement, individuals often can be motivated with an appropriate psychological reward—simply acknowledging the achievement may be sufficient. The most important aspect is to recognize and acknowledge the individual when performance levels have been achieved or exceeded.

Think!
Are you well motivated to achieve your organization's goals? If not, then what has to be done to motivate you?

One way of overcoming motivation problems is to have individuals participate in the planning process. Our systems must be designed to accommodate this. If we put in place a top-down, dictatorial system, then we are more likely to encourage dysfunctional behavior. Individuals who are consulted about their performance targets during the planning process are more likely to see a positive relationship between the organization's targets and their own personal goals, which will motivate them to achieve, or overachieve, to the benefit of both our organization and themselves.

Even with the most participatory of planning systems, it is vital that there is communication throughout the organization. Targets must be communicated in clear terms to those who are expected to achieve them. Individuals cannot be expected to perform against a target they do not know about or understand. Communication of actual results, or *feedback*, is also essential. This task of communication has varying degrees of difficulty depending on the nature and structure of the organization. For small- and medium-sized organizations, it is often a very personal experience as the owners almost certainly will have a much more hands-on involvement in the day-to-day operational activities and hence a much closer relationship with employees. In larger, hierarchical organizations communication has the potential to become more of a problem.

As information, especially planning and performance information, is transferred up and down an organization, the message will inevitably be influenced by the beliefs and preferences of the communicators. This is emphasized in Figure 2.5 by the arrows and hierarchy lines as information moves up and down the organization. There is always a chance that information can be so transformed that it loses its original intent. Employees at the coal face may not always get a clear picture of the objectives originating with executive managers. Likewise, executive managers may lose touch with information originating from the operational hub.

Suffice it to say that designing a planning system involves more than just worrying about how to collect and crunch the numbers. There is a fair amount of organizational psychology that needs to be taken into account as well.

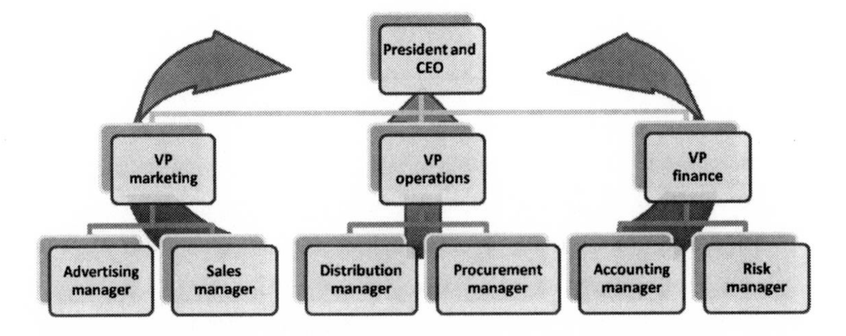

Figure 2.5. Communication channels.

The Preparation of Plans

In smaller organizations formal annual operational guides are actually a rarity. The owners, or managers, likely manage the day-to-day activities of their organization only by reference to a general mental plan. They have a good sense of expected sales, costs, resources, and financing needs. Everything that happens is under their direct oversight, and hopefully they have the mental horsepower to keep things on a logical course. And so it will be, at least in the early stages, for our friends Pearl and Keith. That doesn't mean they should have no formal plan at all. If they don't see any value in preparing a detailed annual operational guide, then they should at least have a strategic plan with which to guide their actions. After all, even in a small organization an authentic business plan will often result in anticipating and avoiding disastrous outcomes.

Medium and larger organizations invariably rely on plans. This is equally true in commercial, government, and not-for-profit organizations. The annual operational guide is an essential facet of the planning and control process, as it provides a formal quantitative expression of expectations. Without it larger organizations are likely to be highly inefficient and ineffective. Nevertheless, the general perception is that the planning process is universally loathed. Why is that so? Simply because it is such a time-consuming process that the information it provides could easily be classified as ancient history by the time it is made available to the functional departments. What is more, most of the people in those functional departments consider the planning process to be an overly financial exercise designed mainly to please the organization's executive management. The result is that no one takes ownership of the process or the product.

Think!
In your organization, is planning welcomed or loathed? Jot down the reasons why.

Let's put that negativity to one side and accept that not engaging in some form of formal planning is not an option. Now let's get on with the first step and think about our strategic plan. Before we actually start to decide on what we need to include, it is worth mentioning that computerized systems help to make the planning process both more meaningful and easier to handle. Probably the easiest system we can use to build our strategic plan is a spreadsheet. For every iteration of our plan we can have just one file that contains many individual sheets, one for each aspect of our plan, which are appropriately linked to avoid problems associated with manually transferring data. Each sheet will have its own model to help structure the relevant data in a meaningful way, so every plan is simply a collection of models into which we shall input some raw data. Computerization will allow easier and faster computation and greater flexibility. We shall be able to explore alternative scenarios much more easily and apply sensitivity analysis much more thoroughly.

Thinking about the future is not an easy task, and as a result a certain amount of error is inevitable. This is no reason to be casual about the estimates that form the basis of our plan. They should be given the most careful consideration, have a rational basis, and be expected logically to occur. Pure guesswork should be replaced by study and statistical evaluation of historical information, as this will give us a good starting point for our predictions about the future. This scientific approach to determining the details in the plan should be applied not only to the elements that are within our own sphere of influence but also to external influences such as changing economic conditions and trends.

The starting point for our strategic plan is the marketing aspect. This will help us focus on what we want to achieve and how we'll go about it. Here we need to start by understanding the environment in which we'll operate and how it will impact on our organization. There are three key perspectives we need to consider here. These are the macroenvironment, the microenvironment, and the internal environment. Marketing specialists will be responsible for looking into these perspectives and providing the necessary data for inclusion in our strategic plan. It is worth understanding, however, why each of these perspectives is important to us.

The macroenvironmental perspective considers all the factors that can influence our plans but that are outside of our direct control. These factors are continuously changing, and so we need to be flexible enough to adapt. The microenvironmental perspective relates to those things that influence our organization directly. They cover all aspects of the relationship and the driving forces that control this relationship between our organization and all our stakeholders. Our understanding of these external perspectives will be better understood by using tools such as PESTLE (political, economic, sociological, technological, legal, and environmental) factor analysis; SWOT (strengths, weaknesses, opportunities, and threats) analysis; and Michael Porter's five forces[2] analysis pictured in Figure 2.6. By considering the internal environment, we shall pay attention to how our plans impact others within our organization to ensure that they are supportive of our initiatives and strategies.

Once the environment is well understood, we can proceed with developing the marketing plan. This will involve a number of steps, the first of which is the setting of marketing objectives. These objectives must be SMART, that is, they must be specific, measurable, achievable, realistic, and timed. The second step is to define our target market: how we intend to position our products or services in that market and what resources we need to do this. The third step is more practical insofar as we need to determine the basic, tactical components of our marketing plan. There are four elements to this: price, place, product, and promotion.

Figure 2.6. Porter's five forces.

These are commonly known as the four Ps, and we have to settle on the weight we wish to give to each of these elements as part of our marketing plan. The final element, as it is with each functional aspect of our plan, is to determine the KPIs (key performance indicators) against which our performance will be measured. We will learn more about this last element later.

Think!
A sound marketing plan is our compass. Do you use one or more of these techniques to develop your marketing plans?

After the marketing plan, which is primarily concerned with which products and services to sell and where, comes the sales plan. This plan is concerned with how that will actually happen. There are two key parts to our sales plan. The first part is about people. What type of salespeople will be needed to achieve our marketing plan, and what will be our expectations of those people? The second part is about process. This requires us to reflect on what systems will be used for dealing with customers, what credit terms will be offered, what payment methods will be acceptable, what warranties will be offered, and what after-sales support will be provided and at what price.

Moving around the planning sequence pictured in Figure 2.3 on page 19, we now need to think about the procurement plan. This is inextricably tied to our marketing plan. Having identified what we want to sell to whom and when, we now need to determine the most appropriate time to buy the products and services at the right price and from the right suppliers to link up with our marketing plan. This is the first obvious sign that our planning process is not a stand-alone event for each functional area but an integrated plan intended to deliver the best possible returns for our organization.

Our operational plan will provide information on how our products or services will find their way to our customers at the time they want them. It will cover aspects such as distribution channels, packaging requirements, delivery costs, and inventory levels.

The administration plan considers all the preceding plans to determine the level of support needed to achieve the targets set by each of the other functional areas. It looks at our organization as a whole to decide what resources are needed in areas such as information technology, human resources, accounting, and general management to ensure that we function on a continuing basis. Planning integration is epitomized in the administration plan.

We are not far from completing our plan because we have reached the end of the sequence, which is the financial plan. Using all the functional plans we shall look at the revenues our organization will earn and the expenses necessary to do that. We'll also need to examine the requests for capital resources, in the form of property, plant, and equipment, which have been identified as necessary to achieve our objectives and evaluate the best way of acquiring them. At this point we shall consolidate all the functional plans, as shown in Figure 2.7, to ensure they form a coherent whole—one that produces an outcome that is both affordable and consistent with our overall strategic direction. If it doesn't, then we'll need to revisit the functional plans and make whatever changes are necessary to produce an acceptable outcome.

Finally, please remember that our plan should be constructed in a way that we as managers can, first, determine if our objectives will be met and, second, compare actual performance against the plans. This second phase, the monitoring process, which we shall come back to later in the book, provides an input into the next planning cycle, enabling us to undertake an informed review and modify, if necessary, our future strategic and operational objectives.

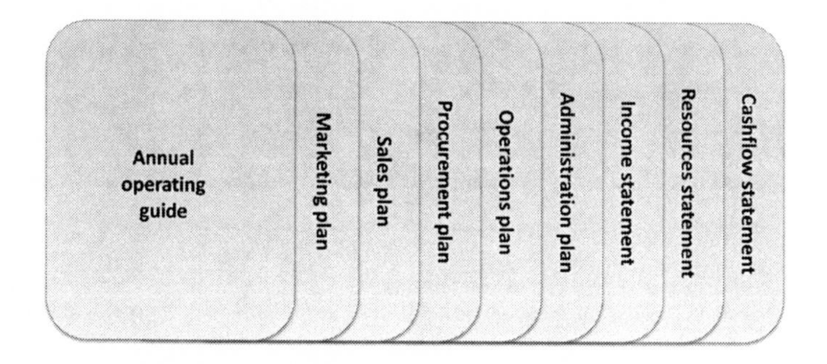

Figure 2.7. Our planning document.

Using Plans for Control

By far the two most difficult tasks in managing an organization are dealing with the uncertainty of the future and coordinating the actions of the various functions within our organization. Financial management practices are sustained within our organization because they provide information essential to its profitable management, in particular information that enables us, as managers, to plan and control operations.

Through the process of setting objectives, broadcasting them throughout our organization, and using them to evaluate results, we are able to improve our control over the organization. Planning may, therefore, be seen as the essential ingredient in control, for without the setting of targets the concept of control is meaningless. To control requires a frame of reference in which performance evaluation can occur, and the annual operating guide provides that frame of reference. Our planning documents are often quite sizeable, however, and contain somewhere around 250 line items, which is too much data for us to monitor effectively. How much data is enough? Working that out is no easy task. Initially we'll probably want to monitor everything, but that will consume valuable time looking in the rearview mirror rather than watching the road ahead. In reality there are probably between 10 and 20 integrative KPIs that will tell us if we are heading in the right direction. We'll have a more in-depth discussion on this topic in chapter 7.

Comparison of actual performance against the frame of reference, with an investigation of the differences, may indicate that control action is required to try and bring the operating performance back into line with the expectations of our plan. It is not always possible or desirable to correct all the differences, particularly if circumstances have changed since the plan was first developed. That said, we should continue to monitor the differences ensuring we understand the reasons for them and modifying our plans where we consider that expedient. On the whole this continuous monitoring process will enhance our understanding of our business environment and allow us continually to refine the planning process each time it is repeated.

Our ability to deal with problems that arise will determine the success of our organization. While no one can foresee the future with perfect clarity, this should be no reason for us to give up the quest to know at

Think!
How does your organization know if it is on the right track? By using lots of specific line items or a handful of well-thought-out KPIs?

least something of the future. We may not be able to find out precise details of the future, but based upon past performance and present operations we are able to construct some of the outlines for the future. To a large degree the clarity with which we see into the future will depend on the tools we use to lift the mist of uncertainty that lies ahead.

Alternative Forms of Planning

What I've described in this chapter so far is considered a traditional historical planning process, which is used in most organizations. It is based on historical information, obviously except in the case of an organization just starting out, adjusted for growth, inflation, and any significant changes in our external and internal environments. It presumes that previous plans reflected organizational priorities that have not changed and were founded on some meaningful justification.

There are three alternatives to the traditional way of developing plans. These are activity-based planning, priority-based planning, and zero-based planning. Each is a viable alternative to the traditional way, and so our choice of planning methodology will depend on our management style. Let's try and understand a little more about each of these other three methods.

Activity-based planning is associated with activity-based costing, something that will be discussed in the following chapter. This form of planning differs from traditional planning in that it concentrates on the factors that drive costs. The volume of activity, for example, will be a key driver of the costs within any of our business functions, and the quality of customer service will have a significant effect on the operating expenses of our sales department. Ideally, our strategic objectives will drive our planning targets and determine the volume of activities to be carried out.

Activity-based planning derives and justifies expenditure plans on the basis of activities carried out in relation to the predetermined cost drivers and places responsibility for cost control on the manager with accountability for the control of the driver. This method separates the analysis of cost-benefit and value of activities from the more mechanistic planning method, reducing the complexity of the planning process and concentrating attention on the management of the organization, not simply on the costs incurred.

Priority-based planning is designed to produce a competitively ranked listing of high to low discrete bids for resources that are called *decision packages*. It is a method whereby all activities are reevaluated each time a plan is produced. Discrete levels of each activity are valued from a minimum level of service upward and an optimum combination chosen to match the level of resources available and the level of service required. This is a particularly good way of linking operating plans with strategy. If priorities change in line with our organization's strategic focus, then new plans will follow those priorities irrespective of historical events.

Zero-based planning is similar to priority-based planning except that it presumes a starting point of zero and identifies expenses that are necessary to implement agreed strategies and achieve the predetermined objectives. It's like we are just starting out without any prior history on which to base our plans. The most important advantage of this method is that all proposed expenditure is judged consistently and that optional and discretionary activities are subject to closer scrutiny. Its most significant drawback is that the required amount of data and number crunching can mean that the effort will obscure the purpose.

Each of these alternative models still views planning as fundamental to the core of our performance and management control structures. There is another option, which is the *beyond budgeting concept*. This model encourages us to focus on beating the competition with aspirational goals for team-based performance. Strategic planning is no longer an annual discussion but a continuous and inclusive process. Equally, rather than prepare an annual operating statement against which performance will be measured, and potentially miss opportunities because they appeared too late for inclusion, resources are made available when needed, improving our ability to deal with the uncertain environment.

Case Study

Planning the Future of Bull-Roo Enterprises Limited

During the week after their Sunday lunch, Pearl and Keith had the first of what would turn out to be many meetings they would have to complete the inaugural planning for their company's future. Those meetings covered each of the three phases pictured in the planning tree (Figure 2.1).

Vision

Pearl certainly had a pretty good idea of what she wanted to achieve with her venture but knew it lacked some focus. The first step was to write their vision statement. Remembering that it needed to be brief and to the point, they decided on the following:

To be the procurer of choice for the wine industry and the door to world markets for their output.

Strategy

They chose the wine industry as their point of entry because it is, by and large, a fragmented industry with many small, boutique wineries requiring common supplies and looking for outlets for their products. They completed a five-forces analysis of their vision and determined the following key strategies as the basis for their initial strategic plan:

- Expand the management team to include expertise in purchasing and logistics.
- Identify key business partners.
- Develop market entry plans.
- Create a web presence as a marketing, sales, and promotional tool.
- Identify an appropriate location for warehousing operations.

This led them to the following key targets to be achieved within the next 5 years:

- annual sales of $200 million
- annual operating profit of $5 million
- sales offices or agents in 10 key markets
- market procurement volume of 65% and sales volume of 35%
- annual shareholder value added of 15% of investment

Operations

Initially, they decided not to expand their strategic plan, which was developed on a staged basis to reflect the progressive achievement of their key targets by the end of their fifth year of operation, into a detailed operating plan. Keith was happy that, for the time being at least, they were able to monitor their performance adequately with relevant KPIs.

Summary

This has been a rather long chapter, but I make no apology for that. Planning is such an important facet of organizational life. Since the financial management function takes ultimate responsibility for the preparation and dissemination of our plans, it is important we understand every aspect of the planning process.

As you can now see, all our plans, and in particular the annual operating guide, are essential tools in translating abstract or general thoughts and ideas into specific action-oriented aims and objectives. If we follow our plans, then the expectation is that the identified aims and objectives will be fulfilled. Abstractions and generic statements, such as "we shall create value for our customers," have no place in our plans. They are management tools and should therefore be measurable, because they provide the benchmarks against which we shall judge success or failure.

Think!
Look at your annual operating guide. What are the key benchmarks? Are they all quantifiable measures, or are some qualitative in nature?

Benchmarks should contain details about how our product or service will be developed, priced, delivered, supported, and financed. The resulting financial performance must be captured and projections for the next few months made. Feedback from operations must be used to refine strategy, refine the medium-term objectives, and sharply focus on the immediate near-term milestones. In short, the strategic and the operational or tactical at times will merge, and so the plans should be the same.

CHAPTER 3

Understanding the Business

Introduction

In the previous chapter we spent a lot of time considering the need for planning as we look to build the road to where we want to be. It was clear that we need to understand how each functional aspect of our organization will contribute to keeping our business in motion as we strive to achieve our strategic objectives. Among other things, this means that we need to know what the cost of our activities will be. But what do we mean by cost?

In the context of our organization, cost may be explained as the valuation in money terms of the effort, material, use of long-lived resources, consumption of utilities, wasted time, risks incurred, and opportunities foregone in making a product or service available to our customers. The key words here are *valuation in money terms*, which puts the responsibility for letting us know our cost of doing business very firmly in the sphere of financial management.

> ***Think!***
> Do you properly understand your cost of doing business? Jot down the key costs as you see them. We'll come back to your list later.

Let's be very clear about one thing. Knowing the cost of doing business in itself will not enable us to differentiate ourselves from our competitors. How we go about our business—our knowledge of all things relative to our organization—is what will make our organization, our products, and our service solutions unique. The way we manage and lead our people and how we organize our operations will determine whether we succeed.

This requires us to make a choice among alternatives, which can be a daunting task. It involves a decision-making process that requires an understanding of the costs attached to each of the alternatives.

To be better prepared for making decisions like this, we need to know more about the different measures of cost, about cost behavior patterns, and about the different ways we are able to establish the total cost of a product or service. Armed with this better understanding, we shall find out more about how we may use our knowledge of costs to assist in choosing between the alternatives we are faced with on a day-to-day basis.

The Elements of Cost

How may an understanding of financial management help us make better strategic decisions? Perhaps the first response to this question is to discourage any attempt to introduce systems that increase bureaucracy. It is far better for us to have information, particularly in relation to costs, that is approximately right than being precisely wrong. The success of strategic actions is just as much a function of judgment as it is of information. Instead of being preoccupied with the recording, analyzing, and presenting of cost data relating to existing activities, we should focus on the provision of cost data about our organization and our competitors that will be relevant in developing and monitoring our business strategy. Such an approach is one of *information orientation*, which starts with a diagnosis of our problems, leading to the structuring of decisions and then to the specification of information that will help in making appropriate decisions.

For all organizations, one of the key essentials in achieving our business strategy is to reduce or contain costs. To attempt this, we first need to know what makes up the total cost of each of our products or services. Then we need to split the total cost into two distinct components so that we are able to understand those costs that are driven by a particular cost object and those costs that maintain our support functions. Let's pause for a moment because I've used some terminology that you may not be familiar with. What do I mean by *cost object*? Many of you will immediately associate this term with the products or services your organization sells. That would be a reasonable starting point. On the other hand, they may not be the prime drivers of the money that you spend. I'm sure that in a number of organizations, especially service organizations like our Bull-Roo Enterprises Limited, it is your customers and their requirements that really drive your cash outflows. If this is the case, then the customer is your *cost object*.

Think!
What is the primary cost object in your firm? Is it possible for us to have multiple cost objects? How might we try to manage that?

Nevertheless, whatever our cost object, we need to break down our total cost into those costs that are readily traceable to our cost object—the *direct costs*—and those costs that are necessary to support our activities but that we are not able readily to trace to our cost object—the *indirect costs*, which are often referred to as *overheads*. Figure 3.1 provides a graphical illustration of where particular costs of a professional services organization, such as a law firm, might lie. In this case the cost object is the customer, whereas in a manufacturing firm the cost objects could quite feasibly be the products that are made. Any item of cost may be either direct or indirect, depending on its traceability to a particular cost

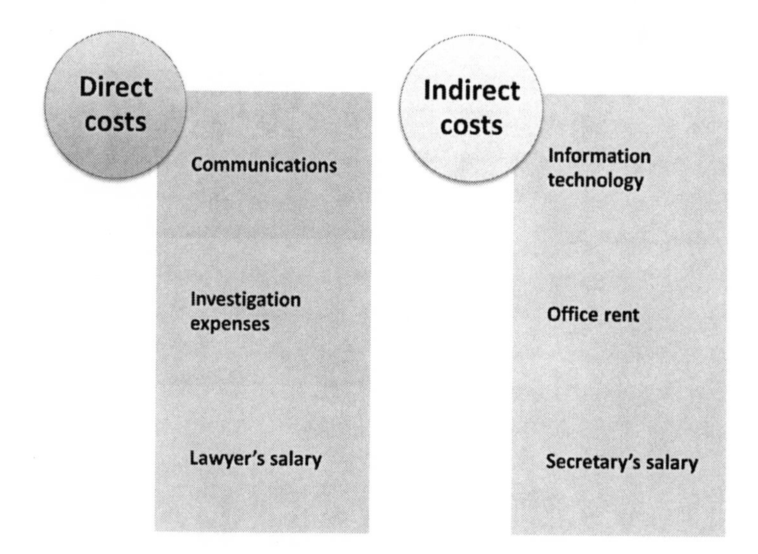

Figure 3.1. Cost elements.

object. As a result of their traceability, direct costs are usually considered to be *variable costs* because they increase or decrease in line with changes in the level of activity of the cost object.

Indirect costs, on the other hand, are more likely to remain unchanged in the face of changing levels of activity and so are considered *fixed costs*. Since it is imperative, in the longer term, that we recover all our costs to remain profitable, it is important that we have some mechanism to allocate these indirect, or fixed, costs to our cost objects in order to calculate the full cost. This process of allocation is a significant problem for many organizations because it is not easy to understand how much of their indirect costs are consumed by their cost objects. If it was understandable, then we would probably consider them direct costs and our problem would go away.

Unfortunately, this arbitrary allocation of indirect costs often results in misleading information about cost object profitability. Indeed, where the cost object is a saleable product or service, some of these indirect costs will be included as a component in the valuation of inventory because they are considered part of the cost of goods sold. Unreliable allocation methods will result in either a higher or lower inventory valuation, which will shift profit between different accounting periods.

From a financial management perspective we should strive to identify as many costs as possible in the direct category, but if we need to understand the total cost of our cost object then we may still be left with the need to allocate some costs depending on our choice of costing system. How should we go about that? Traditionally, the most common methods of allocating indirect cost have been on the basis of a relevant direct input, such as labor hours, machine hours, or units of material. Old traditions die hard, but the nature of our competitive environment is changing rapidly. The ways of old are proving insufficiently flexible to deal with the complexity encountered in our modern organizations.

Let's look at some of the costing systems available to us to see if we can find a model that is suited to our organization.

Think!
How does your organization allocate indirect costs? Is your method really suitable for your business environment?

Costing Systems

Marginal costing—also known as direct costing or variable costing—is the least complicated and most easily understood of the costing systems. It is depicted in Figure 3.2. Importantly, its use relieves us of the problems of indirect cost allocation. Here, in understanding the cost of our cost object, we only include the direct costs. This means that we focus our attention on the contribution, which is the difference between revenues and direct costs that we achieve on the sales we make. Indirect, or support costs, are treated as expenses in our income statement and our target contribution must be sufficient to meet those costs and the required return for our investors.

Absorption costing—sometimes known as total costing—is probably the oldest system of cost accounting in operation. It is depicted in Figure 3.3. It is a system that includes all costs, which means both direct costs and a share of relevant indirect costs allocated on some arbitrary basis, associated with having our product or service ready for delivery to our customer. Even though it was introduced at a very early stage in the development of cost accounting methods, it is still widely used.

Considerable problems are inherent in any application of absorption costing, yet this system continues to flourish principally because it is the only way our organization is allowed to calculate the value of its inventories and, as a result, cost of goods sold for income tax and financial reporting purposes. For management purposes, however, we are free to use whatever method we choose, and that method should be the one best suited to informing us about our progress along the road to meeting our strategic objectives.

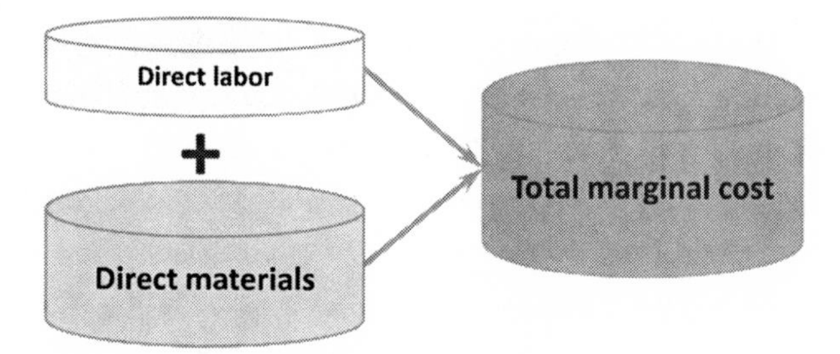

Figure 3.2. Marginal costing model.

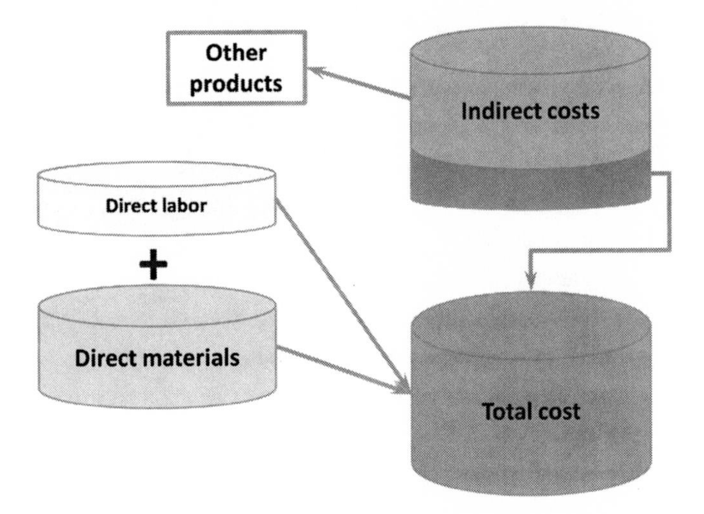

Figure 3.3. Absorption costing model.

The principal conceptual difference between these two systems lies in the treatment of indirect costs. Marginal costing charges it directly against revenue, whereas absorption costing assigns it to productive outputs and thereby includes it in the value of inventories until it is sold to the customer. Proponents of both costing systems recognize that distinctions between direct and indirect costs are valuable for a range of decisions that we as managers will make, and so it seems that the key issue to be resolved is that of timing. When should indirect costs be treated as an expense? At the time they are incurred or at the time they are passed on to a customer by way of a sale?

One of the most significant advances in costing methodology in recent times has been the development of activity-based costing (ABC), shown in Figure 3.4. It is generally accepted that this costing system overcomes the shortcomings of the more traditional costing systems by providing more accurate ways of assigning the costs of indirect and support resources. In so doing, ABC provides a truer picture of what our products, processes, and customers really cost. As with most benefits, this comes at a cost. Critics of this costing system argue that the determination of cost drivers is too complicated and time consuming and that the cost involved far outweighs any benefits that might be derived from improved cost allocation.

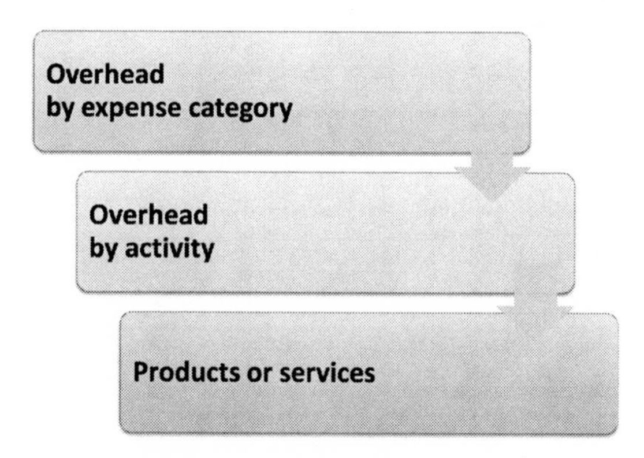

Figure 3.4. Activity-based costing model.

Cost information will always be the basis for most management decision making, both tactical and strategic, but it will always be the activities our organization undertakes that drives its costs. ABC explains how activities consume resources and how products, services, or customers trigger activities. This provides the basis for us as managers to manage the causes (activities) and not the effects (costs) and so be in a better position to assess the value creation to the customer of each and every one of our activities.

Think!
How do you go about costing the products or services that you sell? Does it really help you manage your drivers of profitability?

Many organizations worldwide are now adopting a more comprehensive strategic approach to cost management. A seismic shift occurs when organizations extend their thinking beyond mere price and cost reduction into direct delivery of profitability. There are several alternative costing systems available to organizations that want to take such a strategic approach. Three of them—target costing, life-cycle costing, and kaizen—will be looked at now.

One of the most effective ways we can achieve this is through the introduction of *target costing*, which is depicted in Figure 3.5. Typically, however, there is a lot of confusion in the use of the term *target cost*. It is often applied by design engineers to describe a value analysis or value engineering approach to new product development. An arbitrary cost reduction figure is set, which they then try to achieve. Or it is used as a short-term tactical ploy by buyers in the negotiation process with suppliers. Effective target costing is neither of these.

Target costing is a methodology that leads to the alignment of our customers' perceptions of product or service value and functionality with the design, production, logistics, and cost requirements of our business. Not surprisingly, this cannot be achieved without a fundamental redefinition of our organizational structure away from a functional or departmental perspective. Indeed, the adoption of target costing is a transformational step. It is a strategic approach that is driven by the needs of our customers, with the alignment of our internal processes and external supplier inputs to meet those needs. Target costing is central to the proposition of *value delivery*, whereby customers select a product or service because they believe it possesses a superior value. For this system to work it requires the alignment of all the functions in our organization to deliver customer value profitably.

Figure 3.5. Target costing model.

All products and services go through a typical life cycle, from introduction through growth and maturity to decline. Over time, sales volume increases then plateaus and eventually declines. Our traditional costing systems focus primarily on the time when our product or service is available for delivery to our customers. Unfortunately, this approach often fails to acknowledge the substantial costs we incurred in the design and development phase and almost certainly ignores the costs of discontinuance at the end of the life cycle.

Life-cycle costing estimates and accumulates the costs of a product or service over its entire life cycle, from inception to abandonment. This information allows us to understand whether the profit earned during our products' or services' sales lives covered all the life-cycle costs and helps us to make decisions about future developments. In advanced technology industries, where the design and development phase can commit or lock in as much as 75% of the anticipated total cost as a result of process and technology decisions, this costing model is considered most appropriate.

And so to the last of the costing systems that we'll think about here. Kaizen—改善 that splits into *Kai*, meaning change, and *Zen*, meaning good—is a Japanese term for making continuous, incremental improvements to organizational processes. Kaizen costing, as shown in Figure 3.6, is applied during the sales life when large innovations may not be possible. It focuses on our operating processes, looking for efficiencies in purchasing, production, and distribution. Like target costing, kaizen establishes a desired cost reduction target and relies on teamwork and employee empowerment to improve processes and reduce costs. This approach is based on the premise that employees have more knowledge of the operational processes than managers do.

In considering which, if any, of these costing systems are relevant for our organizational situation, we should remember that if we do not properly understand the cost of making a product or service available to our customers then we are likely to develop inappropriate pricing and marketing strategies. It is not essential to have the most accurate cost system. The aim should be to consistently understand the cost of making a product or service available to our customers, accurate to within 5% or 10%. The idea is to have the most effective costing system, one that balances the cost of errors made from inaccurate measurements with the cost of measurement.

Figure 3.6. Kaizen costing model.

The alternative methods discussed here have widely divergent implications for performance and profit measurement. They also are founded in a different outlook about how we manage our organizations. As we look at each of the systems, we move from a hierarchical view of our organization to one that sees our operational processes as more important in achieving effectiveness and competitiveness. More important, perhaps, are the significant dangers of adopting too rigid an approach to the use of any one system.

Whichever system or systems we choose, consistent misuse could easily result in setting selling prices that will lead us into bankruptcy.

> ***Think!***
> Do you have just one costing system in your organization? If you do, then would it be better if you had a different one for some aspects of your business?

Consequently, our choice of costing systems must be carefully reasoned so that the information we use for decision making will be relevant and useful. Once decided, we need to make a continuous effort to improve the methods of preparing, submitting, and interpreting the information our costing process provides while not being afraid to make changes should it no longer fit its purpose.

Using Costs for Decision Making

Managerial decisions are basically of two kinds: *accept or reject* decisions and *ranking* decisions. Accept or reject decisions arise when we are considering a particular opportunity, acceptance of which will not affect our ability to accept any other opportunities that may become available at another time. It is simply a matter of whether the opportunity will increase our organizational value. Ranking decisions, however, involve the choice between two or more competing opportunities. The need to rank these opportunities arises because circumstances exist that prevent us from accepting all the opportunities that appear to increase our organizational value.

A crucial problem we are faced with is how to identify and evaluate the relevant costs and benefits attached to the various available alternatives. The principles we should apply in determining relevant costs and benefits depend on our objectives. For all decision models, the costs and benefits that are relevant are those that can be affected by the decision. Clearly, if a particular cost or benefit is independent of the decision, then it should not be allowed to influence it. Logically, then, costs that have already been incurred or are contractually committed should not be factored into the decision-making process. This means that only future-oriented costs are relevant. Furthermore, out of those future-oriented costs only those that will differ under some or all of the available alternatives should be considered when we make decisions.

To meet these criteria we need to know which costs change and which costs do not change as a consequence of a particular decision. Identifying the ways in which our costs behave in response to changes in the level of its activities (see Figure 3.7) is, therefore, an important step in trying to determine the effects of particular decisions on organizational wealth. The response of costs to changes in circumstances, including changes in

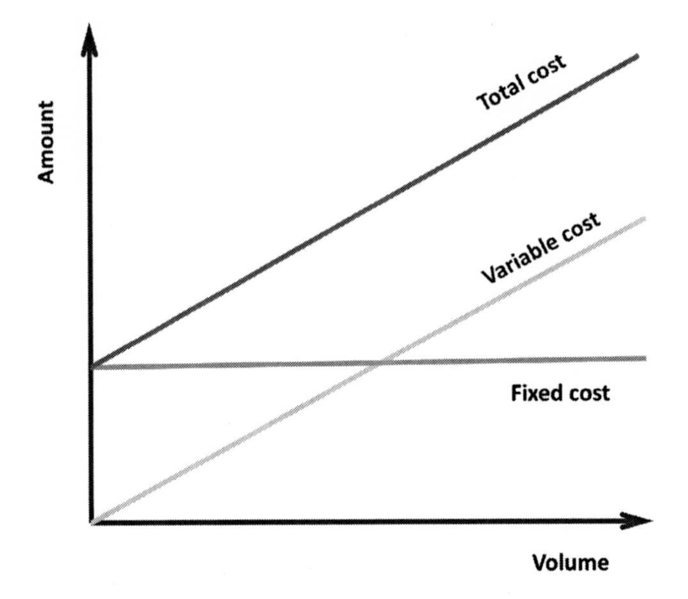

Figure 3.7. Cost behavior.

activity levels, are known collectively as *cost behavior,* and understanding this relationship is vital for optimal planning and decision making.

Unfortunately, real cost data are messy to work with and difficult to use in predicting future events. You may find two assumptions widely used in financial management useful when making cost estimates for any product, system, or service:

- The total cost level should be expressed as a single independent variable rather than by a combination of a number of variables.
- Linear approximations of variable costs are accurate enough even though costs are more likely to behave nonlinearly.

For most cost estimation purposes, approximations based on these assumptions will usually be good enough. Estimating future costs then becomes a simple matter of setting the projected cost against expected levels of activity. Care must be taken, however, because it is usually possible to reliably predict changes in future cost patterns only within a relevant range of activities. Outside of this range individual costs, especially fixed costs, may exhibit changes in their relationship to changes in levels of activity.

Let's consider a straightforward example to make it clear what we mean by relevant range. If we want to provide a service to a client that

Think!
Back to your list of costs. Do you know what happens to them when your level of activity changes? Try to understand that for each of your costs.

takes 1 hour and we can only work for 12 hours in any 1 day, then the relevant range of activity is from 0 to 12 clients each day. Within this range we can service every client who comes to us, and our costs will not change. If demand reaches the critical point, 12 clients, then another staff member is needed, and our cost increases to a new, higher level. This cost then remains constant for a further range of increase in activity, in other words an additional 12 clients, until another staff member is required and another step increase in cost occurs, and so on. If we are to produce acceptable cost estimates, then we must recognize the limitations imposed by the relevant range and adapt our calculations accordingly.

Pricing and Costs

Unreasonably, many organizations continue to approach their pricing decisions in terms of *adding something on to the cost.* Cost in this context will always be the total cost, and so absorption costing continues to provide some information, albeit of an imprecise and significantly inaccurate nature, on which to base a selling price decision. In reality, setting selling prices is concerned with establishing the best price that a prospective customer will pay for our product or service and knowing the lowest price that is acceptable.

The actual cost of providing our product or service, as we have seen, can be determined in one of a number of ways, such as marginal cost, absorption cost, or target cost. By comparing the selling price we think may be achieved with our cost estimate, we are in a position to understand whether making the sale is likely to give us the return we require on our investment in the business. Where we lack accurate or complete market price information for our product or service, our own costs will be helpful in determining a selling price as long as we believe that these costs are typical and competitive. In practice most organizations approach the determination of selling prices through a combination of market research and costing.

On occasions the market selling price will be lower than the projected selling price derived from the cost of our product or service plus the

Think!
Staying with your list of costs, do you use these to set your selling price? If so, then do you know how to modify your prices when volume changes?

margin necessary to provide for an adequate return on our investment. In these situations we shall need to decide whether to do the following:

- Accept a lower price, margin, and return on investment.
- Explore ways of reducing our costs.
- Price on the basis of our cost and accept the probability of a lower margin.
- Explore ways to differentiate our product or service, which is in effect changing our market positioning.

If we decide to explore ways of reducing our costs, then we need to employ kaizen costing and look for ways of increasing efficiency in purchasing, production, or distribution. On the other hand, if we are happy that our cost information reflects reality and that our operational processes are highly efficient, then we have to accept that our competitors, who are selling at lower prices, are willing to accept a lower margin and probably a lower return on their investment. In this situation we need to reflect on our strategy and position in the market.

Price decisions are a combination of market research, competitive analysis, and cost information. In determining selling prices we are attempting to achieve our strategic objectives and return on investment through maximizing our market share, taking into consideration such factors as our own resources and capabilities, competitive prices, market demand, and strategies available, as well as social and legal issues. We supplement these factors by continually monitoring our sales volume, sales mix, and actual performance and feeding the information collected back into our pricing model.

Case Study

Understanding Costs at Bull-Roo Enterprises Limited

Having established their strategy, Pearl and Keith had some things to do quite quickly. The first important task was to identify their initial product range and key business partners. This was Pearl's domain, and she quickly set about creating a plan of action and implementing it.

The second important task fell to Keith since it was his field of expertise. He needed to make some decisions on the costing system they would employ in the business and how that would support the pricing structure. Pearl was pretty sure that their selling prices would mainly be determined by their marketplace and equally that their cost structures would be driven by their customers' attitudes and levels of activity.

Despite Keith's apprehension about the cost of creating it, they decided that an activity-based costing system would be most appropriate for their business since the cost drivers would be reasonably common among their customers. His task now, which was not easy by any means, was to identify each cost pool and the drivers that they would use to determine the cost applicable to each customer.

One of the difficulties they face with this task is that they do not fully understand the activities, and thus the cost elements, of the procurement and distribution function. So they decided to move quickly to employ someone with expertise in purchasing and logistics. Keith had someone in mind from the old days and agreed to speak with him to see if he was willing to join the new venture.

Summary

Costs are the fundamental element in creating value for our owners. Everything we do requires that we reliably understand our cost of doing business. In particular, cost is one of the determinants of the price at which we shall sell our products or services. Just as the price we pay our suppliers—our costs—impacts value creation in their organizations, our selling price impacts value creation in our customers' organization.

Never before have customers so quickly rewarded or so severely punished their suppliers on the basis of value. Today, defining, creating, producing, delivering, and sharing created value comprises an all-embracing framework for every organization. It sets the agenda against which we shall evaluate our organization-wide business development strategies, operational improvement initiatives, and change management programs. Realizing value in our organization and thereby meeting or exceeding the expectations of owners, customers, and other stakeholders must be our overarching aim.

On occasion, the choice between satisfying only our owners or every one of our stakeholders has been tested to the limit. Successful managers realize that over the medium to long term such a forced choice is out of place. The interests of all stakeholders are increasingly entwined, which means we need to pursue value-adding strategies that will satisfy a variety of expectations. Cost reduction programs and pricing activities are vital components of the strategies we pursue, but we should be attentive to the fact that the impact of these activities on our organization alone should not be the only consideration.

CHAPTER 4

Understanding the Risks

Introduction

In the pyramid that is Maslow's hierarchy of needs, an individual's need for security occupies an important place. Our need for individual security is carried over into our working life in several ways. One of these is our desire, although I accept this is not the case for everyone, to avoid the risk of criticism from those to whom, or for whom, we are responsible if our actions can be shown to have adversely affected the life of our organization.

Protecting ourselves against this risk, while enabling our organization to take the right risks, requires an understanding of alternative risks and alternative expectations. It is an attractively simple idea. There are two kinds of risk: those that you are able to exchange away and those that you can't. The only risks people seem to worry about are the ones they can't get rid of, namely the nonexchangeable or market risks. All other risks they accept or exchange depending on organizational policy, if there is one, or their own attitude to risk.

Think!
Before we get stuck into this chapter, what is your attitude to risk? Will you look to take every risk imaginable, or will you look to avoid risk whenever possible? Maybe you'll change your mind when you get to the end of this chapter.

Risk expresses itself in an organization in the variability, or potential variability, in its assets, earnings, and cash flow or in the products or services it exists to supply. As soon as any of these circumstances change, a new set of risks is created, which may be either greater or less than the risk that has been eliminated. Of course, taking risks is a necessary part of conducting business, with returns being the compensation for taking risks. The specter of constant change or the acceptance that risks are a part of our everyday organizational life should not be taken as a reason for doing nothing about risk. At the very least we need to identify all risks that our organization is exposed to whether they are market risks or exchangeable risks. Any action that can economically be taken to reduce an identified risk below our accepted level of tolerance is worth taking. What we must do is evaluate and manage all the observed risks in our organization on a continuous basis.

What might be those observed risks? There are many. Of course, each of them will fall into a particular category. There are risks that arise from the normal course of business, which are operational risks such as the loss of customers, failure of computer systems, poor quality products, and so on. Then there are financial risks, which arise from changes in interest rates, foreign currency exposure, poor credit control, and the like. Many of the risks in each of these categories are exchangeable. Market or nonexchangeable risks are either environmental risks—which arise from changes in external economic, social, or technological factors—or reputational risk that comes from negative publicity, true or not, about our business practices.

Certainly, from a financial management perspective, we are more interested in the risks that fall into the financial risk category, but we should always remember that failure to manage our operating risks is just as likely to result in financial loss. For this reason we need to be involved in the monitoring and management of all the observed risks in our organization.

Managing and Measuring Risk

The global financial crisis originating in the world's financial system in 2007 was caused by failure to exercise management responsibility, above all in the management of risk. This disaster has highlighted the importance of financial risk management to every organization. Yet ironically, it was the development of derivatives by the financial industry as a way for organizations of all hues to mitigate risk in many different areas, a legitimate thing to do, that led to failures in the real economy and a journey down the path toward a global economic crisis.

> ***Think!***
> In your organization, is there a document that identifies all the risks you face and how you manage them? If not, then you need to start one so you'll know what to do about them.

Risk management is not a one-off, notional exercise. It is a crucial function of management that requires commitment and a champion at the executive level as well as chosen employees who have been assigned the responsibility for effective risk management. It is important for us to develop a comprehensive approach to risk management that involves continuous monitoring and review. This continuous process will not only help us to learn from experience and apply a kaizen approach to risk management in our organization but also ensure that all our risks have been correctly identified and assessed, and appropriate controls put in place. All this should be formalized in a risk management policy, setting out our organization's approach to, and appetite for, risk and our approach to risk management.

There are four ways of dealing with, or managing, each risk that we have identified. We can accept, transfer, reduce, or eliminate it. For example, we may decide to accept a risk because the cost of eliminating it completely is too high. We might decide to transfer the risk, which is normally done with insurance or financial derivative products. Or we may be able to reduce the risk by changing the way we operate in our organization. When we have evaluated and agreed on our actions and procedures to reduce the risks to our organization, we need to put practical and relevant measures in place to monitor our situation.

Without measuring risk, how do we know that our risk management actions and procedures are working? How might we go about designing our measurement model? The first step is to identify all our risks and rank them in terms of their significance to our organization. This is best done by considering the consequence and probability of each risk. We shall most likely find that simply assessing consequence and probability as high, medium, or low is more than adequate for our needs.

The next step will be to compare this table of risks with our strategic plan to establish which of the risks may affect our strategic objectives and to what extent. The evaluation process, which may look something like Figure 4.1, should take into consideration legal requirements, stakeholder concerns, impact on the returns from our business, and the cost of mitigation. From this we can determine the significance of the identified risks to our organization and make a decision on whether to accept the specific risk or take action to prevent or minimize it. One thing to bear in mind here is that even though a potential risk may be significant, the cost of mitigating it may be so high that doing nothing makes more sense.

Prioritizing our risks in this way means we are able to direct time and money toward the most important risks. Then, depending on the cost, we can either exchange the risk with another organization or we can put systems and controls in place to deal with the consequences of an event. Sensible and effective risk management will improve the quality and returns of our business.

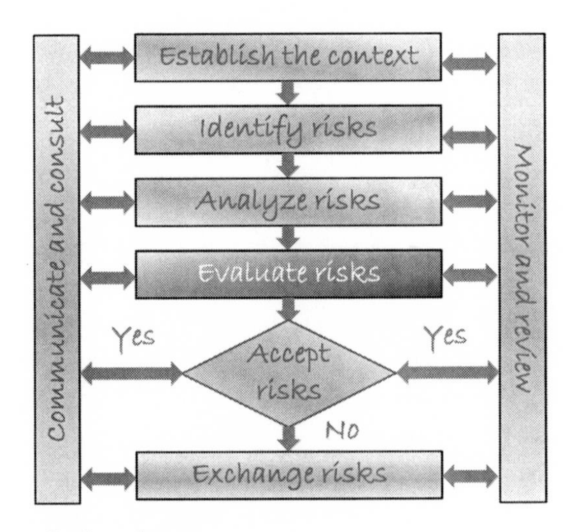

Figure 4.1. **Risk evaluation.**

Operational Risk

Remaining productive, staying competitive, and enjoying continuous improvement means making the best, most informed operational decisions in a timely manner. A sudden and unexpected event, however, may occur anytime to seriously affect the continuity of our business, threaten our image in the marketplace, and impact our shareholder value. Some events result in small but frequent losses, whereas others are rare but crippling.

At an operational level risks are likely to occur in areas such as accounting controls, human resources, information technology and systems, recruitment, regulations, supply chain, and transportation. Using the model described in this chapter and illustrated in Figure 4.1, we should examine each of these operations in turn, prioritize the risk, and make provisions for such an event happening. For example, if we are heavily reliant on one supplier for a key input to our business, then we should consider what might happen if that supplier went out of business or increased its prices significantly and identify other suppliers to help us minimize the risk. If we depend on making and receiving regular deliveries, then we need to think about how we would maintain operations in the event of a fuel shortage.

For many organizations, addressing operational risks is difficult. Insufficient loss data, the lack of established methods for quantifying risk, different types of operational risks with multiple corresponding owners, and an unclear cause and effect of risk and actual incidents are some of the challenges we face. This complexity should not stop us from doing something, anything really, to responsibly handle all aspects of operational risk.

We might not be able to predict when or how the next external calamity will impact our organization, but with the right insight and planning we can better ensure that our organization survives negative events while retaining our competitive advantage. Clearly, then, the success of our business centers on our ability to correctly recognize and successfully manage the risks associated with our operations.

Insurable Risk

Insurance will not reduce our risks, but we can use it as a financial tool to protect our organization against losses associated with some operational risks. This means that in the event of a loss we shall receive some financial compensation, which can be crucial for our organization's survival if it experiences one of those rare but crippling events.

What sort of operational catastrophes is it possible to insure against? Well some events are uninsurable, such as the damage to our reputation, but we can usually find an insurer who will be willing to exchange our risk for a sum of money. There are a number of different policies that are offered to cover operational risks, such as a business interruption policy, an employer's liability policy, a product liability or professional indemnity policy, and a key man policy.

Think!
What insurance policies does your organization have? Are they cost effective? Could you do things differently?

A business interruption policy will cover many adverse events in the daily life of our organization by insuring against the loss of normal operating profit as a result of machinery breakdown or a fire. An employer's liability policy, often required by law, will make it possible for us to meet the costs of compensation and legal fees for employees who are injured or made ill at work as a result of something we did, or didn't do, without bankrupting our company. Similarly, a product liability or professional indemnity policy will protect us against the cost of claims that arise from problems caused by our products or services. Should one of our key employees die, either during working time or at home, a key man policy will provide resources to replace the knowledge and skills that we lose.

The one thing that is becoming very apparent, however, is that insurance companies increasingly want to see evidence that our operational risk is being managed. Also, we shall need to show them that effective processes are in place to minimize the likelihood of a claim. In extreme cases they will not provide coverage. More often they will increase our premium if we are not able to demonstrate sensible and effective risk management.

Interest Rate Risk

Almost every organization is exposed to interest rate risk, although it comes about in different ways. If we have borrowed money at variable interest rates, then our profitability will be at risk when interest rates increase. On the other hand, if we have borrowing costs that are totally or partially fixed, then our profit will be less than it might have been when interest rates are falling. The reverse is obviously true when we are looking at cash deposits. This is the situation that we usually think of when considering our exposure to interest rate risk.

Think!
Where is your organization exposed to interest rate risk?

Changes in interest rates also affect us indirectly through their effect on the overall business environment. In normal times, for example, business confidence rises when interest rates are falling, and we usually experience an increase in our business activity. The reverse is almost certainly true when interest rates are rising. Other areas that will be affected when interest rates change are our employees' pension funds. Falling interest rates will lead to reduced income in the fund. If we have guaranteed benefits, then it means we shall have to pay more into the fund and suffer reduced profit. If we have not given any guarantee, then our employees will see their pension pot getting smaller and are likely to ask for either an increase in our contribution or an increase in their wages so they can put more in themselves. Either way this situation will have a negative impact on our profitability.

As you can see there are a number of sources of risk, both direct and indirect, to our organization from movements in interest rates. We need to make sure that we recognize each of them when developing our risk management model and understand their potential impact on the achievement of our strategic plan.

Interest rate risk is, quite naturally, an exchangeable risk, so we need to understand the instruments of exchange that are available to us if we need them. Most of our possible alternatives are available over the counter, usually from banks, and fall into two groups. The first are those instruments that don't have an explicit up-front premium with the benefits for the counterparty being built into the rates offered. Included in this group are *futures*, *forward rate agreements,* and *interest rate swaps.*

Futures and forward rate agreements are essentially the same, providing a way of fixing interest rates, or unfixing them, over shorter periods of up to 1 to 2 years. The difference between the two is that futures are usually traded on an exchange, meaning they provide us with considerably less flexibility than a forward rate agreement. An interest rate swap is probably the most popular and widely used exchange instrument in the field of interest rate risk. It changes the nature of a stream of interest payments from floating to fixed or vice versa. The market is large and deep with terms of 5 to 7 years common; although, reflecting their different planning horizon, terms of 30 years or more are often used by pension funds.

Caps, floors, and *collars* form the other group, each being a type of option attracting an up-front premium in much the same way as an insurance policy. If we buy a cap, then we'll pay a maximum interest rate over the life of the cap and enjoy lower rates as they come down. Floors are the opposite. We'll receive a minimum interest rate over the life of the floor and enjoy higher rates as they rise. Collars are a combination of a cap and a floor, thus providing us with a corridor of possible interest rates between a minimum and maximum.

The primary advantage in identifying our exposure to interest rate fluctuations is that we are able to minimize possible losses should our understanding of the market be wrong. Unexpected events will be unlikely to disrupt our progress toward achieving our strategic plan. What we must remember, however, is that managing interest rate risk with the instruments described does not eliminate our exposure to interest rate risk; it only minimizes it for a certain period of time.

Currency Risk

As with every other form of risk, the first step in managing currency risk is to acknowledge that such risk exists and that managing it is in our best interest. The next step, unfortunately, is much more difficult. We need to identify the nature and magnitude of foreign exchange exposure. Put another way, what is at risk and in what way?

In many organizations, especially those whose operations are contained within a localized domestic market, managers rarely consider the possibility of currency risk except, perhaps, if they need to source an input or two from another country. Even then, if they are able to negotiate a price in their own currency, then they don't see the possibility of a currency risk at all. This is simply blind ignorance, which is the case here. Nonetheless, it could result in unfortunate consequences. Put yourself in the shoes of the buyer. If the exchange rate between the two currencies changes so dramatically that your supplier, when they exchange your currency for theirs, receives significantly less in their money than they expected, they will be forced to increase their price and so increase your cost and reduce your profitability.

Think!
Are you living in blind ignorance? Where are you really exposed to currency risk?

While most of us think that currency risk is only something that affects organizations buying or selling products or services internationally, as you can see we need to think again. With the never-ending fluctuations in exchange rates of all freely traded currencies, we are probably more at risk that we imagined. *Transaction exposure*, both direct and indirect, is a risk factor in every organization to a greater or lesser extent and something we need to reflect on when developing our risk management model. We must understand the potential impact of currency fluctuations on the achievement of our strategic plan.

Two other forms of foreign currency exposure, *accounting exposure* and *economic exposure*, are particularly relevant to organizations that have assets or liabilities expressed in a currency other than their own. Accounting exposure applies when assets and liabilities denominated in a foreign currency need to be converted into local currency for accounting purposes. The conversion normally results in foreign exchange gains or losses, which impact our profitability. This is of particular concern to organizations that have foreign subsidiaries, but it can also impact organizations that export and import. Economic exposure relates to the overall impact exchange rate fluctuations may have on an organization's value. Even if we only do business domestically, we are faced with economic exposure when our local currency strengthens and improves the competitive position of foreign producers.

Currency risk is, like interest rate risk, an exchangeable risk, so we need to understand the instruments of exchange that are available to us if we need them. There are two methods that we can use to manage foreign exchange risk—*natural hedging* and *financial hedging*—although we may use both methods.

Natural hedging is where we reduce the difference between receipts and payments in a foreign currency by engaging in other transactions in that currency. For example, if we export to countries in the European Union and expect payment in Euro, we could take a loan in Euro and convert it into our local currency immediately and then use the receipts from sales to repay the loan. Natural hedging can be an effective way to reduce our foreign exchange risk, but it can take time to implement natural hedges, and these solutions often constitute long-term commitments.

The other method involves buying foreign exchange hedging instruments that are typically available from banks. The ones most commonly used are *forward contracts*, *currency options*, and *currency swaps*. Forward contracts allow us to set the exchange rate at which we want to buy or sell, on either a fixed date or during a fixed period of time in the future, a given quantity of foreign currency. They are flexible instruments that will allow us to easily match future transaction exposures anticipated in the next year. They are easy to use and carry no purchase price, which makes them very popular with organizations of all sizes. The one constraint, however, is that they create a contractual commitment to deliver to, or purchase from, your bank the agreed quantity of foreign exchange at the agreed future date.

Currency options are other instruments that we can use to mitigate currency risk. Standard options give us the right, but not the obligation, to buy or sell foreign exchange in the future at a predetermined exchange rate. As with interest rate options, currency options attract an up-front premium, but they allow us to benefit from favorable movements in exchange rates as well as to receive protection against adverse movements. Finally, currency swaps, which involve the simultaneous buying and selling of a foreign currency, can help us match receipts and payments in a foreign currency. Currency swaps are simply a combination of a spot transaction and a forward contract. Usually, there are no direct costs associated with the purchase of swaps although some collateral may need to be provided.

Case Study

Risk Management at Bull-Roo Enterprises Limited

Considering the issue of risk in the company, Pearl and Keith were well aware that a significant early risk they faced was their lack of knowledge about the processes and activities, and thus the relevant costs, of the key procurement and distribution function. Keith had someone in mind from the old days and went off to speak with him. They had a long, genial discussion about the opportunity. At the end his friend turned Keith down, although he offered to speak to another person they both knew, Doug, and counsel him to accept the challenge. Within days Doug had agreed to join the team. He started work in 2 weeks. His early tasks would be to contribute to the ABC system development and to identify the operational risks in his area of the business.

Before too long the team needed to sit around the table and identify all the risks that might possibly impact their strategic plan. Intuitively, they knew the risks would be many and varied, but they really needed to understand how each of them was likely to inhibit their chances of achieving their strategic objectives and then to agree whether to mitigate the risk and how.

After a while they completed their review of the potential risks to the success of their venture. From an operational perspective they identified the most important risks as supply chain disruption, product liability, asset protection, and knowledge and skills. Each of these they could exchange with an insurance company for a price. Keith would put more details together and begin negotiations very soon. Since they were not borrowing money to start their venture and did not expect to have surplus funds to invest, they did not see that interest rates were a direct risk to them at the present time. From a financial risk perspective they saw the key risks as currency risk, although they were not in a position to quantify it yet, and credit risk, which related to their concern about receiving payment from their customers when it was due. They agreed to manage the currency risk on an as required basis; but, with limited exceptions, for overseas shipments they would seek payment guarantees from their overseas customers' bankers in the form of letters of credit. Domestic customers could be managed more easily, and they would seek out specialist help for that.

Summary

Every organization has a number of different risks that can be potential threats to its success. Risk management is the practice of identifying and evaluating these potential threats and making decisions about whether we shall exchange these risks, if possible. A risk management model is an important first step in minimizing risk.

Risk is everywhere. If the risk is a calculated one, however, then that's fine and normal. Learn to deal with this fact of life and work with it. On the other hand, there are many risks where the consequences can be destructive. Be aware of them and understand that there are ways and means to protect your organization against them. One way is to ensure that you construct your operational processes to minimize the risk. The other is to exchange the risk with another organization.

Effective risk management is also a matter of using the information derived from risk evaluation to make better decisions and drive growth.

Think!
Are you sure you know where all your risks are now? Time to update your list perhaps.

In this way, risk management is not simply a reactive exercise in protecting value or guarding against failure but a proactive, ongoing initiative directed toward creating value. With effective risk management capabilities we can better coordinate risk measurement, capital allocation, performance assessment, and management across our organization, which will result in improved strategic decisions and increased shareholder value. We have nothing to lose and everything to gain!

PART III

How Do We Get There?

We have begun our journey. So far we understand where we are now and where we want to be in the future. Now we have to understand how to get there. To begin we need some capital. Nothing will happen without the initial investment that on most occasions comes from our own resources. We may have some help, formally or informally, from family and friends; but wherever its source, it will usually be in the form of equity as opposed to debt.

Later when we need more capital to fund the acquisition of resources necessary to expand our markets or increase the products or services we supply or simply to cover the increasing operating requirements as our business grows, we can cast our net wider in search of the necessary funds. Whether we take in additional equity capital or look to finance our growth with debt finance, the investors we approach will need to be sure that our organization represents a sound investment for them.

While financial management may seem arcane and complex to many, there is one thing that you should bear in mind, and this is that an organization's finances and its operations are integrally connected. Our financial structure is fundamentally shaped by our activities, methods of operation, and competitive strategy. The reverse is also true. Decisions that appear to be simply financial in nature may significantly affect our operations. This is particularly appropriate when we are considering the source of additional capital. We must do all we can to ensure we maintain a balance, as depicted in Figure 5.1, that is in the best interests of our organization.

Selecting the most suitable mix of debt and equity is a two-step process. The first step is to decide on the amount of money we require. Frequently, this is the straightforward outcome of the planning process described in chapter 2. We estimate the sales growth, the need for new resources, and the money available from our existing operations. Any

Figure 5.1. Debt-equity balance.

remaining monetary needs must be met from outside sources. If we do not believe we can raise the sum required on agreeable terms, then we need to modify our plans to curtail operations within the funds available.

The second step requires careful consideration of financial markets and the terms on which we are able to raise the additional capital that we need. Whether the source is debt, equity, or a mix of both, we have a tremendous variety of options available to us. Our choices are vital and are at the heart of the financing decision. The proper choice will provide our organization with needed cash on attractive terms. An improper choice may result in excessive costs, financial discomfort, and undue risk to the viability of our organization.

CHAPTER 5
Finding the Money

Introduction

When we are considering how to raise funds for our enterprise, we generally have a choice between equity and debt. It may also be possible in certain circumstances to obtain funds from grants and other forms of government support, especially if we are just starting out in business.

Share ownership, or equity finance, lies at the heart of Western capitalism. By buying a share of the ownership of a company, an investor becomes an owner with a proportionate degree of control over the important decisions. A share is therefore a slice of the action, and the issued share capital is the cornerstone of a company's capital structure. As owners of the company, the ordinary shareholders not only bear the greatest risk in the event of failure but also enjoy the fruits of success in the form of dividends and an increase in the value of their shares. In organizations other than companies, equity is provided in different ways, but the owners still experience the same, perhaps even greater, risks and benefits as shareholders in a company. For sole proprietors or partners in a partnership, a certain amount of equity is contributed and recorded in their capital accounts in the financial records of the organizations.

Other types of shares may be issued by a company. One of these are preference shares, which also constitute a part of shareholders' funds. Shareholders, however, carry no voting rights, except in the case of a proposed liquidation or a takeover. Holders receive an annual dividend usually of a fixed amount.

Debt finance is usually sourced from a bank or finance company, but we can also access the capital markets—an important source of funds with more than 1 year to maturity. These markets exist to channel finance from individuals and organizations with temporary cash surpluses to those with, or expecting to have, cash shortfalls. This critical intermediary function is provided by major institutions, such as banks, insurance companies, and pension funds, which collect relatively small savings and channel them to organizations looking for financial resources. As a result these institutions have become the major holders of securities, both debt and equity, issued by organizations.

In recent years as organizations, particularly companies, have sought to exploit the advantages of each form of capital without incurring the disadvantages, the differentiation between debt and equity has become increasingly blurred by the development of hybrid forms of finance, such as warrants and convertibles. When deciding on the source of any new finance, there are several important factors that we need to take into account. These are as follows:

- the administrative and legal costs of raising the finance
- the cost of servicing the finance
- the level of obligation to make interest or similar payments
- the level of obligation to repay the finance
- the tax deductibility of costs related to the finance
- the effect of new finance on the level of control of the business by its existing owners and on their freedom of action

If we require more capital to finance our activities but don't want to raise additional equity, then we really have only two alternatives: We can sell some of our assets, or we can borrow. Borrowing has a major drawback. If we fail to meet the agreed terms of our loan, especially a scheduled interest payment or principal repayment, then the lender may take legal action to force repayment of the outstanding balance of the loan. Apart from causing financial distress, the taking of such action is likely to harm our reputation. Quite clearly, if we have large amounts of debt, then we run the risk that in a bad trading year we may be forced into insolvency.

Think!
How is your organization financed? Is there too much debt, causing you anxiety? Are the owners demanding more and more? Is it *just right*?

Looking at this more positively, debt finance is always cheaper than equity finance, because lenders assume less risk for exactly the same reason that it is a drawback for the borrower—there is a contractual obligation to repay principal and interest. Also there are major benefits that we can enjoy through borrowing that an astute finance manager can exploit, which include the following:

- It is relatively cheap to raise funds by borrowing. The loan can be syndicated among several banks and other lenders who, by spreading their risks, can offer lower interest rates.
- Interest payments are tax deductible, although this is of value only if we happen to be taxpayers. The ability to set interest payments against profit for tax purposes creates a significant financial benefit.
- Use of debt also imparts a leverage effect where an increase in activity will have a more than proportionately favorable impact on our profit.
- An issue of new equity risks altering the balance of voting control. Debt carries no voting rights; therefore, the only lessening of control is imposed by the inclusion of restrictive covenants, such as stipulations of minimum liquidity levels or maximum dividend payout ratios or restrictions on further borrowing, in the loan agreement.

Forms of long-term debt can be divided into two types: nontraded debt and market debt that can be bought or sold. Nontraded debt originates as, and remains, a contract between lenders and their customers, with a specified interest and repayment profile. It is usually provided by a bank or similar financial institution. Banks offer both short-term advances and long-term loans. An overdraft is the shortest of the short-term advances. It is technically repayable on demand and carries the risk of fluctuating interest rates. A loan may be offered for periods extending to 15 years or even longer for quality borrowers. Repayment profiles are not uniform and are typically a matter of negotiation between the lender and the borrower. When the interest rate on a long-term loan is fixed, and this is not necessarily always the case, the borrower enjoys less risk as well as the advantage of knowing in advance the precise profile of interest and principal repayments.

Market debt is issued in the form of a security, known as a bond, which can be traded on a financial market. There are many different types of bonds, the most common of which are debentures and unsecured loans. These two forms of borrowing differ in one material respect: A debenture is a secured loan. In other words, if the borrower fails to make a scheduled payment of interest or principal, then lenders may take possession of the assets that were pledged as security, arrange for their sale, and obtain repayment of the entire amount due to them from the proceeds of the sale. Otherwise, they are very similar in all other respects. This form of lending normally carries a fixed rate of interest, expressed as a percentage of the face value of the bond, and has a fixed term to redemption or repayment. During the lifetime of the bond, its market value fluctuates with the current rate of interest in the market on debt of a compatible risk. Specifically, if interest rates increase then the market value of existing bonds will fall, and vice versa. As with nontraded debt, borrowings of this nature usually incorporate restrictions on freedom of management action designed to protect the interests of the lenders.

Long Term or Short Term

When, as part of raising funds for its operations, an organization decides to borrow money, the question that is asked first is for how long should it take out the loan? Should the organization be looking to repay the debt in 1 year, 5 years, or even longer? To answer this question, we should understand the reasons why we need the money. If it is for day-to-day operations, then we should consider a short term. If, on the other hand, it is to acquire long-lived resources, then we should be thinking of a longer term.

When we consider our entire capital structure, the minimum risk maturity structure occurs when the maturity of liabilities is the same as that of our resources. If we take this position, then the cash generated from operations over the coming years should be sufficient to repay existing liabilities as they mature. If the maturity of our liabilities is less than that of assets, then we are faced with a refinancing risk because we will not generate sufficient cash from our resources and so we might need to use some of the proceeds from new capital raisings to repay existing debt. The problem here is that there is no guarantee we will be able to raise new capital!

Think!
Have you had problems negotiating a loan rollover lately? Could you do better at matching the term of the loan with the use to which the funds are put?

If the reverse were true, that is, the maturity of liabilities is greater than that of resources, then cash generated from operations will be more than adequate to repay existing liabilities as they mature. Unfortunately, while this approach provides a margin of safety, it may leave us with surplus cash for which we are unable to find a suitable use. If maturity matching is minimum risk, then why do anything else?

Financial Leverage and Capital Structure

One of the key determinants of the rewards available for owners is the financial leverage, or gearing, applied in our organization. We boost our financial leverage when we increase the proportion of debt relative to equity used to finance our activities. Unlike our profit margin where more is preferred to less, financial leverage is not something we necessarily want to maximize even if it does enhance the rewards for owners. Instead, the challenge is to strike a prudent balance between the benefits and costs of debt financing.

By increasing the financial leverage in our organization, we hope to benefit the owners. Hope, indeed, because financial leverage does not always have the desired effect. If operating profit is below a critical value, then financial leverage will reduce, not increase, returns to owners. Let me explain. Replacing equity finance with debt increases fixed costs in the form of higher interest payments. So we need more sales, and thus operating income, to cover this increase in fixed costs; but once breakeven is achieved, distributable profit grows more quickly with additional operating income. To see these effects more clearly, let's look at the influence of financial leverage on our return on equity.

Return on equity (ROE) is calculated by dividing our after-tax profit by the amount of equity. After-tax profit is arrived at by deducting both interest paid and income tax expense from the earnings before interest and tax. Let's start with the situation where our organization is fully funded by equity and has a 12% return on a capital base of $40 million. This means that our distributable profit is $4.8 million. What would be the outcome if we were to structure our capital base in a different way, say $10 million of debt and $30 million of equity?

Assuming our after-tax borrowing cost to be 5%, we would reduce the amount of distributable profit by $0.5 million to $4.3 million. Not so good you might think, but now our equity base is lower at $30 million so our ROE would increase from 12% to 14.3%. Clearly, if we earn more on borrowed money than we pay in interest, then our ROE will rise. The opposite, of course, is equally true, causing a worse performance when things are not going so well. If we think of the increased variability in the return to owners brought about by borrowing as an increase in risk, then it would be fair to say that financial leverage is a two-edged sword: It provides greater returns to owners, but it also increases their risk.

The Cost of Capital

The cost of capital is the rate of return that we pay our investors to compensate them for providing funds, and it reflects the risk they take. It reflects the average of the cost of debt and the cost of equity weighted in their market value proportions and represents the rate of return we must earn on the resources employed in our organization to meet the expectations of both debt and equity investors.

The cost of debt is easy to work out. It is the cost of borrowing from lenders. As a very rough approximation, the cost of debt is the interest rate payable on it. There is, however, a further aspect to consider: Tax relief on debt interest is usually available to organizations. Because of this, the effective cost of debt to our organization will be less than the nominal cost as long as we have sufficient taxable profit to absorb the interest cost. If, for example, our bank will lend us some funds at 7.5%, the after-tax cost, assuming our rate of tax to be 35%, will be 7.5% × (1–35%) = 4.9%.

Although not quite as easy, it is possible for us to work out the cost of equity by reference to the expected future dividends we shall pay on our shares. It is a valuation model that considers dividends, and their growth, discounted to current values. This model works on the basis that the valuation of shares is based on these things:

- current dividend
- future growth in dividend
- required rate of return

Without boring you with the arithmetic details, the present value of the assumed dividend payment stream, at a discount rate of K_E, is

$$P = \frac{d}{K_E - g}$$

and, solving for the discount rate,

$$K_E = \frac{d}{P} + g$$

This equation says that if our assumption about perpetual growth in dividends is correct then the cost of equity is the same as our company's dividend yield (*d*/*P*, where *d* represents the next dividend payment and *P* the current market price of one share), plus our expected annual growth rate in dividends. If, for example, our current share price is \$7.20 and the next year's dividend is expected to be \$0.25, which reflects a consistent average growth rate of 6% annually, then the cost of equity can be calculated at (25 ÷ 720 + 0.06) = 9.5%.

Think!
Can you work out your cost of equity this way?

As you can see, this model works only if a current market price exists for our shares and if we pay a dividend. For many organizations this isn't possible, and so we need to find an alternative approach to work out the cost of equity. One such method is the capital asset pricing model (CAPM). This approach builds on the idea that the rate of return required by equity investors, and thus the cost of equity capital for an organization, is made up of a risk-free rate of return plus a risk premium associated with our organization. Finding out the risk-free rate is fairly straightforward if we accept that the returns from government bonds can be used as an approximation. A more difficult problem, however, is working out the risk premium for our organization. CAPM does this using a three-step process:

1. Obtain the risk premium for the market as a whole.
2. Compare the return for our organization with the return from the equity market as a whole.
3. Apply this relative measure of return to the risk premium for the market as a whole.

The first step is easy. We can obtain the yield on 30-year U.S. treasury bonds to use as the risk-free rate of return. Today it is 4.2%.[1]

The next step is to obtain the return from the equity market as a whole, which is currently estimated to be 5.4%.[2] By taking the risk-free rate from this expected return we arrive at a risk premium for the equity market as a whole of 1.2%.

The third step is a little trickier, because we need to know our organization's *beta*. This represents the relative measure of return that we are looking for in step two of the CAPM process. For companies listed on a stock exchange their beta is readily available. For other organizations, while it is possible to engineer a figure for their beta, it is not such an easy task.

Just to complete the exercise, I obtained the beta for Cisco Systems Inc.[3] On November 20, 2010, it was 1.25. To obtain the risk premium for Cisco, we simply need to multiply the market premium by Cisco's beta—1.2 × 1.25 = 1.5. This we add to the risk-free rate of 4.2% to give a cost of equity for Cisco of 5.7%.

For many organizations it isn't possible to obtain either a market price for equity or their beta risk index, and so we are better off letting history be our guide. An approach to estimating the cost of equity along these lines, which is generally more successful for organizations whose equity is not publicly traded, starts by looking at the expected returns on risky investments. In general, the expected return on any risky asset is composed of three factors: the risk-free interest rate, an inflation premium, and a premium for risk. The first factor is compensation for the opportunity cost of holding the asset, the second is compensation for the declining purchasing power of our investment over time, and the third is our compensation for bearing risk.

Fortunately, we do not need to treat the first two factors separately because together they are the same as the expected return on a default-free investment, such as a government bond. Since it's easy to find out the government bond interest rate, the only challenge we are faced with is to estimate the risk premium.

Let's start with the yield on 30-year U.S. treasury bonds as the most suitable government bond interest rate, which I indicated earlier was 4.2%. Now we need to add our reward for bearing the extra risk. Again, using information provided earlier, this is 5.4%. Together they yield an estimate of 9.6% as the cost of equity capital for a typical organization.

To work out our organization's cost of capital, all that remains now is the figure work. If our organization has $1 million of debt, representing 20% of the total investment and $4 million of equity, the other 80%, then the weighted-average cost of capital (WACC) is $(4.9 \times 0.2) + (9.6 \times 0.8) = 8.66\%$. This means that we need to earn at least this percentage return on the market value of our resources to meet the expectations of our investors.

Think!
OK, time for you to try and work out your weighted average cost of capital. Good luck!

Working Capital Management

Working capital is the name given to the difference between the short-term resources, commonly known as current assets, that we own and the short-term funding, or current liabilities, that we use to support those resources. Typically, the value of our current assets exceeds the value of our current liabilities, which means that working capital represents an investment. As with any other investment, we should invest in working capital only if it will generate a return greater than could be obtained from alternative investments.

Because of the close relationship between the day-to-day operations and the continual change that occurs in the makeup of current assets and current liabilities, it is most likely that a greater proportion of the finance manager's time will be spent managing working capital than on any other aspect of the business. The reason for this is that successful management of the working capital cycle is fundamental to the financial well-being of our organization and is an important element in the overall financial planning process. You can see why it is important that you are able to understand the main elements of working capital and the working capital cycle.

The compound that is working capital is made up of four ingredients mixed together in the following way:

Working capital = inventories + receivables + cash − payables

Inventories, receivables, and cash are some of the normal components of current assets, and payables are one element of current liabilities.

As far as inventories are concerned, it is important to realize that there are different types. One core distinction we make is between product-related inventories and service-related inventories. The former are directly related to the earning of revenue while the latter are for various support functions and include such items as maintenance and office supplies. Production inventories include stocks of raw materials, work-in-process, and finished goods. They might also include, especially in the case of a wholesaler or retailer, inventories purchased simply for resale. In all cases the investment in inventories is made to support the income earning activities of our organization whether that is production, selling, or support. The level of inventory held ought to be sufficient to ensure that each activity generates the necessary contribution to our overall profitability but no more than that.

For the most part receivables arise from selling on credit terms to customers who have not yet paid the amounts they owe to our organization as a result of those sales. They may also arise, however, from other forms of transactions, such as the granting of short-term loans. Why do we offer credit terms to our customers? Usually, it is to secure sales that we might not otherwise obtain. The extent and terms of credit that we offer are a result of market positioning decisions and will frequently be influenced by the customary practice of the market in which we operate. There is a balance to be struck here, which is the one between the additional profit generated by extra sales and the cost of financing the resultant investment in receivables and, of course, the potential cost of default by customers.

Organizations need ready access to cash to enable them to fund their day-to-day payment obligations and to deal with unexpected contingencies. Maintaining liquid cash resources including bank current accounts, however, means that these resources are not being used for productive investment and are not providing the returns that such investments do. It means we have to strike a balance between the benefits of the liquidity and flexibility afforded by holding cash and the associated cost, in particular the opportunity cost, of the foregone returns from productive investment.

Payables are the converse of receivables. They represent the short-term credit that we have obtained from business partners in our supply chain. Payables may also include short-term finance from lenders, such as bank overdrafts, as well as money due to employees for unpaid salaries, to government agencies, and to the providers of employee benefits. It may seem like this short-term credit appears costless, but there are often hidden costs, perhaps related to our overall relationship with suppliers, which really need to be taken into account. We need to reconcile the cost of short-term funding, both apparent and hidden, with that of other types of funding as well as with the return that is generated from the investment made with these funds.

Think!
How long does it take you to convert payment for an input cost into cash from a customer?

There is no question then that we need to evaluate every one of the costs and benefits associated with each element of working capital. Some of these costs and benefits may be difficult to quantify in practice. Nevertheless, we really must make a sensible effort on that front so that we optimize the use of funds within our organization. The concept of managing our investment in working capital is relatively straightforward: Invest in short-term assets as long as they generate a return greater than the cost of capital, and use short-term sources of finance as long as they have a cost lower than other sources of capital.

Cash Planning and Management

From what I said before it's easy to appreciate that cash is more than just one of the elements of working capital. It is the medium of exchange and a store of value. As such it provides the linkage between all the financial aspects of our organization, and so effective cash management is vital to every organization irrespective of size. The key to this is effective management of the working capital pressure points of payables, receivables, and inventories.

Most organizations will hold a certain amount of cash. The actual amount tends to vary considerably depending on the nature of our business and our ability to borrow money quickly. If we can do that, then the amount of cash we need to hold can be reduced. It's the same if we have some resources that are easily converted into cash, such as investment securities or government bonds.

To manage cash effectively it is useful for us to prepare a projected cash flow statement. This will enable us to see clearly how planned events are expected to affect the cash balance. The projected cash flow statement will identify periods when cash surpluses and deficits are expected. This information can be incorporated into one of the several models that have been developed to help us control our cash balance.

My preferred model suggests the use of upper and lower control limits for cash balances and the use of a target cash balance. This model, pictured in Figure 5.2, assumes that either we have some marketable securities that can easily be liquidated if we need access to cash or we have an agreed loan facility from our bank, which can be drawn down or repaid as we need.

If our cash position exceeds either of the limits, then we have to decide if the cash balance is likely to return to a point within the bands within the next few days. If this seems likely then no action is necessary. If, on the other hand, we can't see this happening, then we must change our cash position either by buying or selling marketable securities or by repaying or drawing on our loan facility. This model relies heavily on our judgment to determine where the control limits are set and the period within which breaches of these limits are acceptable. Past experience is really useful in helping us decide on these issues.

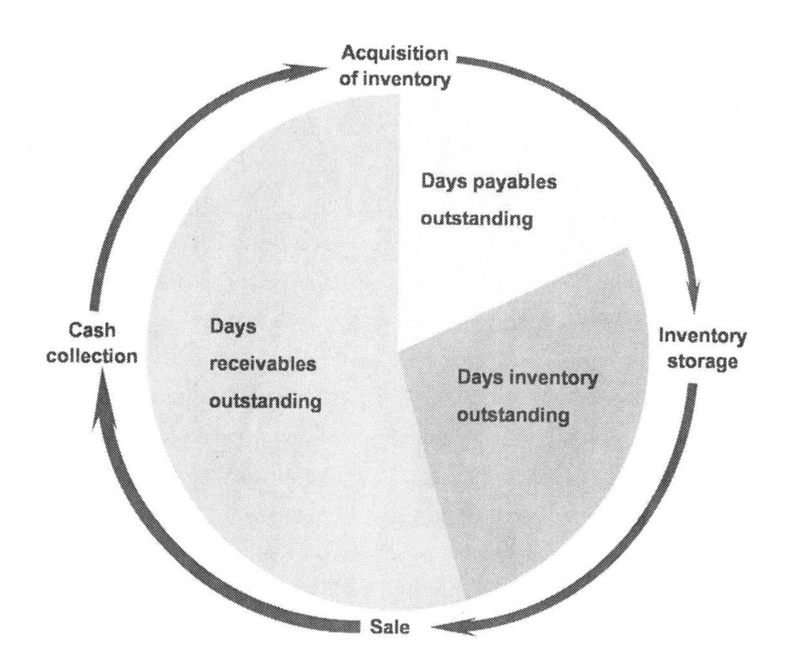

Figure 5.2. Calculating the operating cash cycle.

When managing cash it is important that we are aware of our operating cash cycle. This is quite easy to calculate as can be seen in Figure 5.2. For a retailer, for example, it represents the period between the outlay of cash necessary for the purchase of inventories and the ultimate receipt of cash from the sale of the goods. Understanding our organization's operating cash cycle is important, because it has a significant influence on our financing requirements. Broadly speaking, the longer the cycle the greater our financing needs and therefore the greater our financial risks. For this reason we should be trying to reduce our operating cash cycle to the minimum possible period.

Case Study

Finding the Money for Bull-Roo Enterprises Limited

With Pearl's initial equity contribution the company has a sound financial base on which to start out in business. Keith added some more equity when he agreed to join forces with Pearl. Doug will also buy some shares once he has been with the company for 12 months. If everything goes according to plan, then they have enough capital to see them through the first 3 years of their business life.

Once they get to the fourth year though it's a different story. Their planned rate of expansion means that they will require additional investment in the company. Keith analyzed the options available to them, and they have decided that the investment they need in the fourth and fifth years of operation will be best sourced from lenders. So Pearl once again contacted old friends to sound them out about providing some medium- to long-term loans in a few years time. She gave them a copy of the strategic plan, and they agreed to consider the possibilities. A few days later Jenny, who manages investments for a pension fund, rang Pearl and told her that her pension fund would be prepared, in principle, to provide the loans that their plan suggested they might need. Closer to the time they would negotiate a mutually satisfactory agreement. Great. Things couldn't be progressing better.

The long-term side of things was organized for the present. Now it was time to focus on the short-term issues, and one of those was their working capital projections. These looked OK, but they were concerned about getting paid on time by their customers. They saw credit risk as the most important risk their company faced. They planned to overcome this by asking for letters of credit, with limited exceptions, from their overseas customers. For domestic customers Keith negotiated an arrangement with a reputable factor not only to look after credit management activities but also to purchase 90% of their receivables within 48 hours of the sale. The balance of 10% would follow when the customers had settled their accounts. They have not only minimized credit risk but also ensured an improved and stable cash flow.

With the arrangements now in place they would have no problem meeting payment arrangements asked for by their suppliers as long as they could manage their inventory cycle within the number of days provided in the plan. Doug was supremely confident that this would not be a problem, and he even had some ideas about how that could be significantly improved. He would try them out once he started negotiating with suppliers for the goods they needed.

Summary

Every new organization needs money when starting out. Many will need to buy equipment, establish a workplace, and meet marketing costs—all before the first sale is made. Then once the organization is under way, it needs cash to pay the bills and keep the organization going.

We have a wide choice of financing options when starting up, and choosing the right ones for our needs is essential. We can use our own money, borrow from banks, family, and friends, or attract outside investors. Grants and government support may also be available. Most businesses use a combination of these alternatives according to their specific needs and circumstances.

Once we've been going for a while, apart from looking to external sources for additional funds, we are able to raise funds, both short and long term, internally from our cash flow. From a long-term perspective, keeping earned profit in our organization really helps when it comes to funding needs. Looking at the short term, the control of cash and the selection of an appropriate working capital strategy that supports our overall business strategy will help prevent unexpected cash problems.

The choice is ours. We just have to make sure that we find the most beneficial and prudent balance between debt and equity sources of funds that provide us with the lowest possible cost of capital to go forward with our bright ideas.

CHAPTER 6

Is This the Right Idea?

Introduction

The chief determinant of what our organization will become in the future is the investment we make today. Our strategic objectives will not be achieved unless we outlay money today to receive benefits in the future. We need to regularly generate and evaluate creative investment proposals that will enhance our competitive position in the environment in which we choose to operate. A key step in this process is the financial evaluation of these proposals, which is frequently called *capital budgeting*. Here we decide, first, whether the anticipated future benefits are large enough, given the risks, to justify our investment and, second, whether the proposed investment is the most cost-effective way to achieve what we want to achieve.

We have already seen that organizational life revolves around raising funds from various sources, which is then invested in resources to produce a return greater than the cost of funds. These investments require outflows of cash and will subsequently generate inflows of cash. It is the nature of things that these cash flows, both out and in, do not all occur at the same time. Often the time lag between them is considerable. Investment opportunities that we consider usually involve a relatively large outflow of cash initially followed by a subsequent stream of smaller cash inflows. Selecting which investment opportunities to pursue and which to avoid is a vital decision because individual projects often involve relatively large and irreversible commitments of funds that extend for a considerable period of time.

Costly and far-reaching mistakes can, and probably will, be made unless we exercise great care when making an investment decision. This starts by understanding how such decisions are best made, which requires a clear appreciation of the various methods available for us to use in evaluating and deciding about potential investment opportunities. As part of this learning process we must recognize that there are significant differences between the theoretical appeal of particular techniques and their popularity in practice.

There are several different models that we can use to assess investment proposals. Some are relatively simple and rely on standard accounting figures. Others, taking into account the old adage that *a nearby cent is worth more than a distant dollar*, employ discounting. Viewed broadly, the discounted cash flow techniques considered in this topic are relevant whenever we contemplate an action involving costs or benefits that extend beyond the current period. This covers a lot of ground, including such disparate topics as deciding between sales channels, analyzing property or equipment acquisitions, deciding whether to launch a new product, choosing among competing manufacturing technologies, valuing divisions or whole companies for purchase or sale, assessing marketing campaigns or research and development programs, and even designing corporate strategy. Indeed, it is not an exaggeration to say that discounted cash flow analysis is the backbone of modern financial management and even modern business.

Think!
How do you decide whether to invest in projects or long-lived resources? Do you ever check to see if things worked out the way you expected?

In this chapter, the various investment appraisal techniques are scrutinized along with how they may be used to determine whether we should proceed with an investment or some other business opportunity. Along the way we shall also consider the problems of risk and uncertainty and examine how we can accommodate uncertainty in our investment appraisal activities.

Evaluation Techniques

How we go about evaluating investment opportunities partly depends on the type of decision we have to make. To begin, we should consider a quick and simple evaluation to decide whether a project is worthy of further examination. After this initial screening we need to subject the opportunity to more extensive scrutiny to decide whether the project meets our investment criteria. This leads us to the last step where, usually because we have limited funds available for investment, we need to choose between competing projects to ensure we carry on with those that promise the greatest wealth creation.

We have a number of techniques available to us, which fall into one of two groups—those that employ discounting techniques and those that don't. The key thing to appreciate is that only discounting techniques fully recognize that money received today is more valuable than money received tomorrow because we can put it to work earlier, which makes discounting techniques more appropriate for evaluating longer term investments.

Before we look at each of the techniques available to us, it is worth a paragraph or two to identify what information we need to include in our evaluations. Our investment opportunities will result in costs being incurred and benefits being received later. We must focus only on the *relevant* costs and benefits, which are those that will not be incurred or received if we decide not to proceed with the project. Usually, these are only costs and benefits that result in a future cash flow. There is one important exception to this, and that relates to opportunity cost. Here there is a good chance that no cash changes hands because we are talking about something that is given up or foregone. As an example, an opportunity cost of full-time study is the salary that you could have earned if you had been working instead. The lost salary is not a cash flow, but it might have been.

On the other hand, there are some costs that may result in a future cash flow that are considered *irrelevant* to the decision process. These relate either to costs to which we are contractually committed, and are therefore inescapable, or to apportioned fixed costs that would have been incurred anyway. Be careful here, because if the project leads to increased fixed costs then any incremental overhead should be considered in the evaluation. One last thing to mention is that all costs and benefits that have already been incurred or received will have no bearing on the investment decision, as it is not possible to change the past.

What about our evaluation techniques? The first is simplicity itself and is the most common way that we undertake the initial screening of opportunities. This is known as the *payback* method, which tells us how quickly we recover our initial outlay from the cash flows generated by the project. For example, if a project requiring an investment of $3 million expects to generate annual cash flows of $1 million, then it will pay back the investment after 3 years. If our criterion demands a return of cash after 4 years, the investment would be acceptable. On the other hand, if we are expecting a 2-year return, then we would not proceed further with our investigation. This technique is biased in favor of quick-returning projects and so provides a safeguard against two forms of risk: those of total market collapse and organizational failure because of illiquidity. The technique is simple and understandable. The notion of how quickly we get our money back is a powerful one.

The second nondiscounting technique uses accounting data rather than cash flows. This is a well-used technique because it is based on terms familiar to most businesspeople, such as *profit* and *capital.* What's more, it is consistent with the way many of us are rewarded—according to the return on investment achieved—making it the forward-looking counterpart of our reward concept. We're talking about the *accounting rate of return*, which uses accounting profit as the numerator and investment as the denominator in a calculation that is usually expressed as a percentage. The accounting profit is the annual cash flow less the annual depreciation charge, which is the annual allocation of cost over the useful life of the investment. The most common way to express the accounting rate of return is to calculate the average annual profit over the project's lifetime and then to express this as a proportion of the initial outlay. The project will be acceptable if the calculated accounting rate of return exceeds some specified target.

This leads us to the discounting methods. As well as focusing on cash flows, these methods all have the common advantage of incorporating the rate of return required by our investors. A project is only worthwhile if it generates a rate of return greater than that. Many organizations ignore this simple truth and end up destroying value for the owners. The first of the discounting methods is the *net present value* method. The first step with this method is to establish the future cash flows for each time period, usually 1 year. Before moving on to the next step it is important to understand two golden rules that apply when calculating the net present value:

1. *Do not deduct interest payments from the operating cash flows.*

   The operating cash flows reflect the investment decision, while the discount rate reflects the financing decision. By discounting we are finding out whether our investment proposition is able to tolerate our cost of finance. If we were to include expected interest payments in our calculations then we would, in effect, be double counting for the cost of finance.

2. *Depreciation is not a cash flow.*

   Depreciation is simply an accounting adjustment that allocates the initial cost of a resource over its expected lifetime. The relevant cash flows for evaluating an investment proposition are the cash paid when purchasing the resource and the cash received, if any, when selling it. If we were to include depreciation in our calculations then we would, in effect, be double counting for the initial outlay.

We then discount these cash flows at the rate reflecting the return required by our investors and add the results to obtain the gross present value of the future cash flows from the project, which we compare to the investment required to undertake the project. If the gross present value exceeds the outlay required, then the net present value is positive, which indicates the project provides a return greater than that required by our investors. On that basis we should go ahead with the project.

There is a mathematical formula that we are able to use to calculate the present value of a cash flow at some future date. You probably don't need to know that, so I'll not elaborate here. If you know how to use spreadsheets in Microsoft Excel, the formula to use is = NPV. On the other hand, tables with discount multipliers for round number percentages are readily available. A shortened one, covering periods up to 10 years and discount rates from 1% to 20%, is included in this book in appendix 1.

Think!
There are a number of choices here. Which, if any, do you use? Do you use more than one method? Why?

There are two variations on the net present value theme. The first relates to a situation where the expected future annual cash flow is constant. This stream of cash receipts is called an *annuity*. So rather than discount each of the future year's cash flow, we are able to use the table in appendix 1 that relates to the present value of annuities. Here we simply multiply the expected annuity by the factor applicable to the discount rate and the number of years that we expect to receive it.

Sometimes we expect our annuity to continue for an eternity. This gives us the second variation on the theme, which is a *perpetuity*. These can be straight or growing, and each has a slightly different method of calculation. To determine the net present value of a straight perpetuity, we simply divide the expected cash flow by our discount rate. For example, the present value of a perpetual cash flow of $100 at 10% is (100 ÷ 0.10) = $1,000. If we expect that cash flow to grow each year then we are talking about a growing perpetuity. Here we use the same approach except that we deduct the expected annual growth rate from the discount rate we apply. So using the previous example, if we expect our $100 to grow by 2% each year then we would apply a discount rate of 8%, which is the required 10% less the expected growth rate of 2%, producing a present value of (100 ÷ 0.08) = $1,250.

There are times when, due to a lack of funds or other resources, we can't proceed with all the investment projects that meet our criteria for acceptance. We need to rank them starting with the opportunity that provides the greatest return. To help us with this we are able to use a *profitability index*, but it is not the most effective method of ranking. Let me explain, starting with how the calculation is performed. It is quite straightforward. We simply divide the gross present value by the initial outlay. Since we are considering only opportunities that have a positive net present value, the result of this calculation will always be greater than 1. The result is representative of each project's efficiency in terms of the capital invested at the start. This method has one significant drawback, and that is it doesn't make an allowance for projects of different durations. So if we have two opportunities that give us a profitability index of 1.5 but one project will last for 3 years and the other for 5 years, how do we rank them? Using this model they are equal, but intuitively we know the one with the shorter time span is more effective. Nevertheless, this method provides us with a ranking that is biased in favor of relatively productive projects, which is something we should be grateful for. If opportunities are that close as we get toward the end of our funds or resources, then a closer inspection of the remaining projects should ensure we select the one with the shorter duration.

This leaves us with just one more model to consider, and that is the *internal rate of return*. Put simply, this is the discount rate that produces a net present value of zero. The decision rule is to accept opportunities where the internal rate of return is greater than the cost of capital. It will always give the same answer as the net present value method to our evaluation of opportunities. That said, since this is perhaps the most complicated of the models available to us in terms of calculation, we should stick with the more straightforward option. Nevertheless, the internal rate of return method does resolve the problem of ranking opportunities as it provides us with the annual percentage return over the life of the project.

The Treatment of Uncertainty

While we spend quite a lot of time looking in the rearview mirror of our organizations, we also spend time looking into the future. When we engage in planning, we do. When we evaluate investment opportunities, we do. In every case, the biggest problem we face is that we don't really know how realistic our expectations of the future are. In the short term this may not matter too much as we are able to quickly rectify any mistakes in our estimates, but when it comes to investment opportunities, faulty estimates have the capacity to inflict great harm on our organization. Much of this problem arises from the sheer unpredictability of the future.

Human nature says we shall pay more attention to the negative possibilities, which may lead us into talking ourselves out of a perfectly good investment opportunity. As shown in Figure 6.1, the uncertainty of the future is like a coin: There are two sides, and we should always bear that in mind. There are times when things turn out better than expected. So a sensible way of looking at the uncertainty surrounding our projections of the future is to think about the positives as well as the negatives: Is our glass half full or is it half empty?

What's the best way of treating uncertainty? We need to use our insight, experience, and judgment to make canny assessments about the

Figure 6.1. Two sides of uncertainty.

relative likelihood of different outcomes. It is unlikely these guesses will have any objective underpinning, and so they are called *subjective probabilities*. Even so, they have a useful role to play if we accept them as rough-and-ready guides to particular situations.

Let's think about an investment opportunity that is dependent on market demand, such as the construction of a new hotel. Our evaluation of the project has indicated that in a stable market the net present value will be \$3 million. We think the chance of this being the case is 40%. If we see an increase in tourist arrivals then there's a chance we shall see a better return from the project, a net present value of \$5 million, but with economic conditions the way they are the likelihood of this is only 15%. The balance of expectation, that is, 45%, is that there will be a continuing deterioration of the market, which will produce a negative net present value of \$1 million. All we need to do now is determine the expected net present value of the project. This we do by weighting each possible outcome by its probability of occurrence, like this:

$$\{(3 \times 0.40) + (5 \times 0.15) - (1 \times 0.45)\} = \$1.5 \text{ million}$$

The expectation is that our project will still have a positive net present value, and so it should proceed, unless there is a competing project that will offer a greater return over a similar lifetime. Knowing the expected net present value does not make the decision; it only summarizes information about the possible outcomes.

Risk and Return

Most of us are well aware that all financial decisions involve risk as well as return. By their nature, investments require the expenditure of a known sum of money today in anticipation of uncertain future benefits. So when we are evaluating investment proposals, we need to incorporate considerations of risk as well as returns. There are two such considerations that are especially relevant. First, when we are evaluating a particular investment opportunity, risk impacts our ability to estimate relevant cash flows. Second, and perhaps more important, risk itself enters as a fundamental determinant of investment value. Put this way, if two investments promise the same return but have differing risks, then most of us will choose the one with the lower risk. Why? Because we are averse to risk. You and I, as risk-averse investors, will not entertain high-risk investments unless they offer greater rewards.

This risk-return trade-off is an important consideration in most of our decisions. While we look to see if our proposed investments will provide a return greater than our cost of capital, we really should ask ourselves if the return is sufficient to justify the risk. How are we going to estimate the amount of risk present in an investment opportunity? In many situations the amount of risk may be calculated objectively from scientific or historical evidence. More often, though, investment propositions are unique and estimating the risk is a subjective process. In this situation we depend on the perceptions of our colleagues, their knowledge of the environment, and their understanding of the investment's ramifications. Once estimated we need to incorporate risk into our investment decisions. The most popular and practical way of doing that is to add a premium, which reflects the perceived risk of the project, to our cost of capital to give us a risk-adjusted discount rate that we can use in our calculations.

Case Study

Decision Making at Bull-Roo Enterprises Limited

The team is progressing well. Many things are now in place, but there are some crucial long-term decisions that need to be made. One is relatively straightforward. The company needs somewhere to call home and that includes a place to warehouse the things it proposes to buy and sell. The others, which relate to different product lines, are somewhat more complex.

Let's look at the premises situation first. Doug has been looking around for somewhere suitable and has identified two possible locations. One is available only to rent, whereas the other could either be rented or purchased outright. He has collected all the relevant data and calculated the net present values of each of the options. The rent-only option has a net present value of minus $1.25 million. The other choice gives a net present value of minus $1.43 million for the rent option and minus $1.18 million for the purchase option assuming they take out a loan to cover 60% of the cost and repay it over 10 years. Each of the options is minus because we are considering outlays only, and so we should be considering the smallest negative. It is the purchase option on the second property. Pearl is not particularly happy about this as she really doesn't want to start borrowing money until the business has found its feet. They discuss their choices at some length and finally decide to rent the first property as long as they are able to negotiate a suitable lease. Keith goes to talk with the owner and comes back with a 10-year lease with an option to purchase at the end of the lease. Another good result for the fledgling company!

The product line evaluations, on the other hand, are quite mixed. Indeed, it is not an easy process as they are unable simply to eliminate those that do not offer sufficient returns without there being a negative impact on one of the other lines. They apply several simulations around product mix and finally come up with a package they believe the growers will accept. With heavier weighting on minimal market growth and increased competition, the expected net present value is only just positive. The team feels that they've considered the worst possible position, and they can still get the returns they need. It's all systems go now. It's time to start negotiating contracts to buy and sell at both ends of the supply chain in their chosen industry, the wine industry.

Summary

In this chapter we have been thinking about how we know if we have the right idea. An important part of this is knowing how to evaluate possible investment opportunities. The models put forward are useful tools to assist in making decisions of a long-term nature. Often, however, decisions in principle are made subjectively before we seek to justify them by the application of financial techniques. Nowhere is this more apparent than in a start-up organization where there is little experience on which to base projections of future cash flows.

Indeed, projecting the future with any degree of certainty is fraught with danger even in the oldest of organizations. Yet even if you have a lot of confidence in the data collected and the models applied, then reliance on financial techniques alone will quite often fail to capture the richness of the different ideas put forward to enhance the future of our organizations. Proper technique is never a substitute for thought, work, or leadership. Always remember people, not analysis, get things done.

PART IV

How Do We Know That We've Arrived?

It is all very well to plan our journey, but we need to understand how we are progressing toward our final destination and, ultimately, whether we have arrived where we intended. Financial statements of different hues are a crucial ingredient in helping us here. We are not the only ones who are interested in the success of our journey. Along the way we are helped by all sorts of interested parties, and, naturally, they are quite keen to see that we are successful for the rest of the way.

The list of those who are interested in our progress, which we can tell them through our financial statements, seems to grow longer by the day. Some of those people are directly connected with our organization, for example, our employees; others are not directly connected, but they may be affected by our financial stability, such as our business partners in the form of customers and suppliers.

Given the wide range of interested parties and the diversity of their information needs, it should not come as any surprise that we provide a wealth of information in our financial statements. For all those outside our organization we provide them with statements that report on our financial performance for a given period of usually 1 year, identify our financial position at the end of that time, and explain where we got our money and where it went to in that time. In general terms these statements help to provide the answers to three basic questions about our organization:

1. What return is this organization making?
2. What is the risk associated with this organization?
3. Does this organization have sufficient cash?

Basically, someone reading our financial statements should be able to answer these questions.

While these statements are also useful for us, they provide only information in aggregate form. We need a lot more information and in considerable more detail than we provide in our public statements to help us understand where we have been and what we still need to do to reach our destination. Monitoring progress needs to occur more frequently than once a year, and often to explain a unique event. To satisfy this need the reports we provide internally often give a forecast as well as historical information and are constructed in a way that is useful to us.

Think!

Yikes! Are you inundated with financial statements as well as pages and pages of notes? Do you really need all that information? Can you absorb it all?

Being provided with information in the form of financial reports is, by itself, inadequate whether we are external or internal users. We need to understand what this information means, which requires analysis and interpretation. The analysis is normally couched in the form of a comparative measure, such as profit relative to resources employed, as an example. Interpretation means making a judgment about the worth of that measure, and this is often done by comparing the result for our organization against an industry benchmark, another organization, or even the performance of our organization over time. Nevertheless, making comparisons and drawing conclusions from financial information has inherent risk, and we should be careful to look at other aspects of organizational performance at the same time.

CHAPTER 7

Measuring Business Performance

Introduction

Organizational performance should never be evaluated in isolation. For example, what does a test mark of 40 really mean? Is it good or bad? No one can say unless they know the desired level of attainment and the maximum number of marks available. If we want to get more than half marks and the maximum possible mark is 40, then perfection has been achieved. On the other hand, if the maximum mark is 100, then we have been unsuccessful in our endeavor. The same applies to organizational performance. A number of predetermined performance targets enables the effectiveness of activities to be evaluated.

Various measurement criteria may be adopted, but the important performance indicators are those that identify the degree of achievement of our strategic objectives. This means that we must have suitable measures in place, reflecting the core values of our organization. More importantly, the monitoring and reporting mechanisms we use should be designed to focus people's behavior toward achieving our objectives. The resulting common sense of direction fosters the necessary team effort required to produce the best possible outcomes. Of course, this is just looking internally at our performance. There are outsiders who are equally interested in how our organization is performing.

The information we provide to outsiders is pretty much defined by a universal understanding of what is considered important. A regulatory framework is evolving to guide and control the content of publicly available financial information so that there is clear and consistent communication between an organization and its stakeholders. How recipients use that information is up to them, but they would normally be making economic decisions regarding their relationship with our organization.

Simply looking at the figures provided in the financial statements will not help. We need to look behind the numbers to better appreciate the setting that produced these results. Most organizations provide descriptive elements in their reports, such as the directors' report, and reading these helps to put the performance into perspective. Using this contextual information and a more detailed analysis of the financial information, we have a clearer picture of the past performance, financial strength, and future prospects of an organization.

What's Really Important?

Our performance measurement system is what tells us whether we are on the way to reaching our strategic objectives. These objectives will change from time to time to reflect changes in the world in which we operate. This means that our performance measurement system should be in a state of constant review that will probably result in frequent changes to ensure it remains aligned with our strategic objectives. Failure to do this will cause employees to continue to reflect on things that are now less important while not focusing on what is newly important. Since we comprehend only what we measure, our organization's inertia will keep it moving in the same direction it had been going should we fail to change measurements.

Evaluating our performance involves the use of either objective or subjective performance measures, or combinations of both. Objective criteria include explicit, verifiable measures, such as sales, profit, or value added per employee. Subjective criteria focus on multiple hard-to-measure factors. For example, subjective performance measures of a manager include a variety of factors, such as improving team spirit, getting along with peers, and meeting targets and schedules. Most organizations will use a mix of objective and subjective performance measures to ensure that their team does not focus entirely on the objective criteria to the detriment of their other responsibilities.

Performance measurement systems generally use both financial and nonfinancial measures of performance. In the past we have tended to focus our assessment of performance on tactical operations. Where we are faced with a constantly changing landscape, our ability to link operations with strategy and then assess whether we are getting it right has been coming up short. As Michael Hammer[1] says,

> In the real world, a company's measurement systems typically deliver a blizzard of nearly meaningless data that quantifies practically everything in sight, no matter how unimportant; that is devoid of any particular rhyme or reason; that is so voluminous as to be unusable; that is delivered so late as to be virtually useless; and that then languishes in printouts and briefing books without being put to any significant purpose . . . In short, measurement is a mess.

Numerous performance measures divert our attention from the things that matter. We need to identify several key indicators that will articulate what it is that we need to get better at if we are going to reach our destination. Importantly, some things have a greater effect than others and so we must explicitly specify the relative weights for each indicator when they are used to assess performance. As you can see, it is important that performance measurement reflects our strategic direction and that the reporting of performance properly compares actual achievement with the intention of our strategy.

Think!
Is your performance measurement system a bit like Michael Hammer describes—a mess? What can you do about it?

General Purpose Financial Statements

The many users of published financial information need to be confident that it truly reflects the reporting organization's financial performance and financial position. For this reason a system of regulation has evolved to guide and control the content and presentation of published financial information. For many years these regulations were developed for local use by local regulators. In the United States there were the pronouncements from the Financial Accounting Standards Board. In Australia they came from their own Accounting Standards Board and in New Zealand from their Financial Reporting Standards Board. In the United Kingdom the Accounting Standards Board of the Financial Reporting Council produced their Statements of Standard Accounting Practice. Now there is a coordinated approach to the development of these regulations through the International Accounting Standards Board.

Most organizations publish three financial statements, usually annually but sometimes more frequently. These are the income statement, the statement of financial position, and the statement of cash flows. Their purpose is to inform external stakeholders who rely in some way on the organization whether the organization has a long-term future, whether it is financially stable, and what sort of return could be obtained from an investment in it. This is what we see through the first set of eyes, and so the statements are not that relevant or useful when we are trying to plot our way through an environment filled with opportunities and dangers.

Management Reporting

In a commercial setting our strategic decisions determine our competitive market position, and for this reason, they are the most important decisions we shall make. It follows that the value of information is potentially higher in relation to strategic decision making since the cost of mistakes is so much greater, and so the importance of providing relevant and timely performance related information should not be underestimated.

Creating, understanding, impacting, managing, serving, manipulating, and exploiting markets are the common denominators of organizational strategy, which is nothing without implementation. There are two key elements in the drive for profitability. One is the ability to maximize revenues, and the other is the effort to reduce or contain costs. In relation to the first, an absolutely crucial feature of our success is the ability to position our products or services within the marketplace in a way that generates an acceptable and sustainable profit margin. This calls for full recognition of the impact on, and relationship between, the prices that our customers are prepared to tolerate and the level of appropriate functionality that is being provided in meeting their needs. The relationship between pricing and functionality is crucial. Furthermore, it impacts the likelihood of being able to maintain high levels of profitability, the probability of competitive attack from other organizations, and the linkage with necessary operational improvement strategies to reduce or contain costs, such as target costing.

A well-designed performance reporting system focuses on results and measures these results against objectives and targets that have already been established. How well these results measure up is a key element in evaluating our chances of reaching our destination. What is more, it will have everyone pulling in the same direction, since we are all working toward the same objectives. Unfortunately, when it comes to our organization, a good reporting system will not turn a poor performer into a good performer. It may, however, turn a good performer into an even better performer, because the information provided encourages people to strive for the best.

To discover whether we have a good performance reporting system, a number of questions need to be asked. First, are the reports being read and acted upon? Reports distributed without any feedback are an indication that the system is not highly effective. Indeed, they may not contain information that is relevant at the time. Second, do the reports provide sufficient information for us to take corrective action where necessary without delay? Internally, the main purpose of performance reporting is not to tell us where we have been but, more importantly, where we are going. If this kind of information can't be gathered from the reports, then they are simply not doing their jobs. Third, are we receiving the information we need in a timely fashion? Knowing we have a problem only days or sometimes weeks after it first becomes apparent simply isn't good enough. We are well endowed with technology these days to ensure our performance reporting is on-line and in real time. What is more, a good performance reporting system must have credibility, which it gains by being accurate, fair, and clear. What does each of these entail?

Think!
Do you still produce reams and reams of paper reports each month? Who reads everything? Can you convert to real-time, on-line reporting?

When we say our system must be *accurate* it does not just mean that the numbers must add up but also that any mistakes in the system must be corrected without delay. There is nothing more discouraging than for mistakes to carry on after they are noticed and reported to the finance manager. If the mistakes persist, users will simply ignore the information.

By *fair* we mean that cost allocations should be made on an equitable basis. Overhead must be distributed in such a manner that those receiving a portion of it understand the basis of allocation, and while they may not like it, they should recognize that there is no fairer way possible to distribute the burden.

The reports, or other information, we provide should be *clear*, which means that they must be quickly and easily understood. Reports should not require further analysis or additional calculations on the reader's part. One of the best ways of presenting clear reports is through charts and graphs. This type of visual presentation is easier to read than columns of figures, and graphics keep people interested in the presentation. Further, as we make more use of technology the information provided in an on-line and real-time way should be presented as a graphic in much the same way as the instruments in our cars.

As always there are other things that we can think about. Perhaps the most effective way of presenting performance information is through exception reporting. Exception reporting works on the premise that we are usually flooded with too much information and have difficulty extracting the important things from the dross. By highlighting information that is out of the ordinary, and not reporting on those items that are within established parameters, we can concentrate on what is important.

Even if we limit the amount of information that is distributed throughout our organization to that which is necessary for managing our strategy, there will still be plenty to digest. Not everybody needs to know everything, and so individuals should receive only information on which they can take action. This means that reports *for information only* should be eliminated wherever possible in the interest of reducing the information glut. For example, status reports that are created during a crisis should be eliminated once the crisis has passed.

The most important factor in designing performance reporting is to know your audience and to present them with the information they need and want so that they are able to manage effectively. More often than not, readers of reports prefer to see summaries and conclusions with detail being provided only when an item moves outside of its established

Think!
Do you get information that may be interesting but not directly related to what you do? How do you sort out the wheat from the chaff?

parameters. What is more, there is no point in giving individuals information about something over which they exert no influence.

Apart from performance reporting we often prepare reports that provide important information to assist in making a decision. When presenting information that will be the basis for significant policy decisions, such as opening or closing an office or deciding to enter a new market, it is imperative that we clearly present information that will describe and discuss the benefits and drawbacks of all the options and alternatives that are available to us. If a recommendation is requested, then we should present it and make it clear that this is our opinion. Of course, it is necessary to support our conclusions, and the analysis that does this is included as an appendix to the report.

Reporting for management is a complex and often thankless task. Each manager requires something different, but this should be expected in the diverse ecosystem that is our organization. As you have seen there are lots of things that we must consider when developing a performance reporting system, but most of all it should emphasize our organization's strategy and the key initiatives chosen to achieve it. Choosing the most appropriate performance measures, like measuring those things that individuals can influence, will help everyone see more clearly how the work they do contributes to our results. Traditional reporting and performance measurement systems are becoming less fashionable as they rarely approach this vital activity in a strategic, forward-thinking way. Strategy mapping and scorecard measuring are the way of the future.

Balanced Scorecard

In today's environment, an organization's journey is no longer on a long, straight road. It winds around bends and traverses hills that don't allow much visibility or certainty about the future. We must be agile and continually transform our activities and their cost structures. This is difficult to do when the people who matter most in our organization, our front-line employees, do not understand our strategy, the relevant performance measures, our cost structure, and the economics of our environment. It is much easier to engage with a kaizen-style transformation process when we link measures to strategies. Failure to do so will create misalignment of our cost structure and priorities with our strategy.

To avoid this hole in the road we need to improve our communication. Ideally, everyone in our organization should be able to quickly answer this question: *How am I doing on what is important?* We can be of assistance by providing the tools that will help them align their work with strategy. Scorecards will do this because they express the strategy in measurable terms, communicating what must be done and how everyone is progressing.

Yet here we need to be careful. Are we constructing a scorecard or a report card? Will it be used for punishment and reward, or for causal analysis and collective remedy? There is a distinction. Report cards are part of the accounting police work. They are used to determine who has been good and who has been bad. Sure, responsibility and accountability are important but not as important as uniting our organization in the quest for success in our journey. If we do not want to simply make harsh judgments but rather monitor performance to generate feedback communications about what needs to be changed, then we should look seriously at developing a scorecard system.

There are a number of different versions of scorecards available, although the most popular is the *balanced scorecard.* This scorecard, shown in Figure 7.1, recognizes the importance of both financial and nonfinancial performance measures as it examines our organization through four different but interrelated perspectives:

1. *Financial.* How is success measured by the owners?
2. *Customer.* How do customers see us, and how do we create value for them?
3. *Internal.* What is the short list of internal processes, procedures, and activities at which we must excel to satisfy customers and owners?
4. *Learning and growth.* What changes in employee capabilities, information systems, and organizational climate are necessary to continuously improve our internal processes and customer relationships?

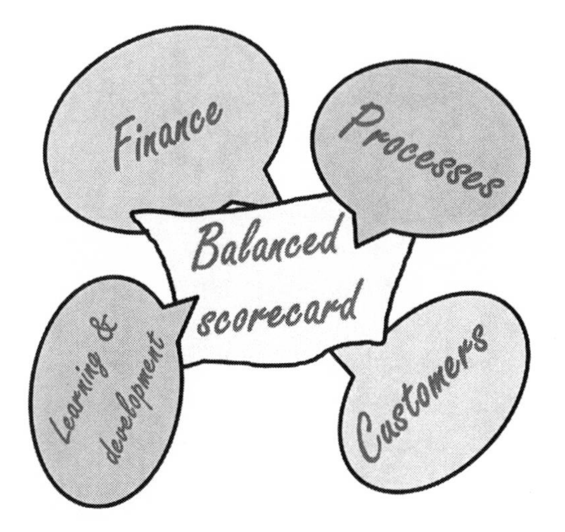

Figure 7.1. Balanced scorecard concept.

Key performance indicators in each of the four perspectives of the scorecard should be directly or indirectly related to each other. Let's follow that logic. Our organizational strategy is the starting point and dictates the financial perspective objectives. To achieve the financial perspective objectives we need to look at our relations with customers and determine how we can add value for them. The source of added value is the efficient and quality working of internal processes. Processes cannot operate efficiently, however, without appropriate learning and innovation within the organization. Identifying these links is critical to implementing a successful balanced scorecard, which in turn is critical to understanding progress toward achieving our objectives and mission.

Think!
Do you use something like a scorecard in your organization? If not, then could you?

Case Study

Performance Reporting at Bull-Roo Enterprises Limited

The company is only just starting out and is run by a small team of hands-on owners. They all understand the strategy and what needs to be done to meet their targets. Do they really need a performance reporting system?

There is no question that they are obliged to produce general purpose financial statements for use by the outside stakeholders. Keith will take care of those in the fullness of time. But what do they need for themselves? One thing is for sure, they don't need to be swamped with meaningless data. That is, of course, entirely up to them. During one of their morning discussions the question of performance reporting was raised. All of them agreed that some form of scorecard reporting was the preferred way to go, and they opted for the balanced scorecard model. They intended to try and implement an electronic version that would be updated in real time. Obviously, a software package was needed, and they agreed to consult their information technology business partner on that.

Understanding the connectivity of the perspectives in the balanced scorecard, they began to think about the key performance indicators although they were a little perplexed about where to start. What they did know was that they didn't want too many indicators to look at. From a financial perspective their key indicators were clear. They were interested in the return on invested capital, the profitability of customers, their ability to generate cash, and their ability to add value. How that linked with their relationships with customers was not too hard, and they decided on a customer satisfaction indicator, a settlement indicator, and a demand indicator. They identified the key internal processes as their delivery performance, their sourcing ability, and the efficient issuing of paperwork. Measures would be developed for these activities. That left the learning and innovation perspective to be filled. Clearly one area of importance was their ability to find new and better ways of doing things, so they agreed that one measure would relate to the introduction of effective innovation. The other key area was their ability to translate tacit knowledge into explicit knowledge and how it would be shared among them. How to measure performance in that area required a little more thought, but when they had worked it out that would complete the first version of their balanced scorecard.

Summary

Increasingly, we, as managers, are being blamed for poor organizational performance. The problem doesn't just relate to planning and execution systems; it is much more a problem of communication and culture. Often we judge performance by monitoring too many outcomes with some measures being outside our influence and control. On top of that, the information we are supplied with is typically reported too late, too financially weighted, and not predictive. We are swamped with too many after-the-fact measures that inadequately summarize too much information.

Think!
Is your organization's performance measurement system reactive or proactive?

The evolving management philosophy of strategy maps and scorecards evokes immediate appeal because of its fundamental message—excessive focus on financial results is unbalanced because nonfinancial measures influence eventual outcomes. This means that we need more nonfinancial measures being reported on an ongoing basis rather than at the end of some arbitrary accounting period.

Performance management, through the use of a well-designed performance measurement system, creates a shared vision that will allow us to effectively manage our strategic objectives in a way that maximizes value to all stakeholders. We need to project just one version of the truth because a single version will allow us to optimize organizational efficiency, support continuous improvement, and maximize the value of our human and capital resources.

CHAPTER 8

Analyzing Business Performance

Introduction

The mythical reader of financial statements takes many forms and has been the subject of many studies. Establishing the identity of the end user of financial reports is important for those who design accounting systems because they seek to provide an output of information, the scorecard of performance, which is going to be timely and relevant to the needs of the reader.

To many people lacking in financial knowledge, the general purpose reports produced by any accounting information system represent a mysterious collection of numbers that have a semblance of authority and an implied degree of accuracy. For these people the image of reports is further distorted by misconceptions resulting from the accounting methods applied and a lack of appreciation as to the depth of information that may be gleaned from the financial statements.

Someone with knowledge of accounting understands that the financial statements supply information about our organization's profitability, the amount of investment in long-term resources, the level of working capital, and the sources of finance. They do not, however, give direct answers to these questions:

- Is the level of profit adequate?
- Are the owners reasonably rewarded?
- What financial problems face the organization?

It is only by analyzing the information contained in our financial statements that we are able to answer these questions and, at the same time, improve the quality of information flowing between the reports and the readers. That's why the skills of financial analysis are important to a wide range of people, including investors, creditors, and regulators. But nowhere are they more important than within an organization. Regardless of functional specialty or company size, anyone who possesses these skills is able to diagnose their organization's ills, prescribe useful remedies, and anticipate the financial consequences of their actions. Clearly, if you do not fully understand accounting and finance, then you are working under an unnecessary handicap.

Let me provide an analogy. The cockpit of an A380 jet looks like a three-dimensional video game. It is a sizeable room crammed with meters, switches, lights, and dials requiring the attention of two highly trained pilots. When compared with the cockpit of a single-engine Cessna, it is tempting to conclude that the two planes are a different species rather than distant cousins. But at a more fundamental level the similarities outnumber the differences. Despite the Airbus's complex technology, the pilot controls the plane in the same way the Cessna pilot does: with a stick, a throttle, and flaps. To change the altitude of the plane, each pilot makes simultaneous adjustments to the same few levers.

Much the same is true of organizations. Once you strip away the façade of apparent complexity, the levers with which we affect our organization's performance are comparatively few and are similar from one organization to another. Our job is to control these levers to ensure safe and efficient progress and, like the pilot, remember that the levers are interrelated. We cannot change the organizational equivalent of the flaps without also adjusting the stick and the throttle.

The Need for Comparison

Examining the relationships between values reported in the financial statements of an organization is considered a fundamental way of analyzing business performance in a number of areas, such as profitability, asset management effectiveness, liquidity, financial leverage, and investor returns. Most organizations have key ratios as part of their strategic objectives and goals against which actual performance is monitored. Similar forms of analysis are also used by analysts, bankers, and investors as an aid to investment decisions.

Just calculating a ratio will not tell us very much about that particular aspect of our organization. For example, if our A380 jet consumed fuel at

> ***Think!***
> Do you compare or benchmark performance in your organization? Is it just an exercise, or do people take notice of the results?

the rate of 3 gallons per mile, then it would not be possible to work out from this information alone whether this particular level of performance was good, bad, or indifferent. It is only when we compare this ratio with some benchmark that the information can be interpreted and evaluated. What possible benchmarks could we use to compare this ratio?

There are, in essence, three possibilities: past performance, similar organizations, and planned performance. By comparing the ratio we have calculated with the same ratio, but for an earlier period, we can understand whether there has been an improvement or deterioration in our performance. Tracking a particular ratio over a longer period allows us to identify trends in performance. To be successful our organization needs to perform better than our direct competitors. To find out whether we are we should compare a particular ratio with the same one from our competitors. We can also compare actual ratio calculations with the targets that we set as a way of revealing the level of achievement attained.

Ratio Analysis

As part of the process of understanding what is happening in our organization we can calculate ratios that convey information on certain relationships in the financial statements and compare the changes in those relationships over time and against our competitors as well as industry averages. The number of ratios that may be calculated is endless; yet we need only to work out a few to highlight the usefulness of financial analysis. The mere calculation of a ratio is of itself meaningless; however, used with care and imagination, the technique can reveal much about our organization and its operations. It is useful to think of ratios as clues in a detective story. One or even several ratios may be misleading, but when combined with other knowledge about our organization and the environment in which we operate, ratio analysis can tell a revealing story.

Most ratios fall into one of five categories. These are designed to provide information about *profitability*, *asset management effectiveness*, *liquidity*, *financial leverage*, and *investment*. In each of these categories there are some standard calculations that have proven useful over time. It is not necessary to think only of these as there may be other, more useful comparisons that we would like to make. The key is simply that the comparison is relevant and useful and that the data we need to complete the calculation are available. Let's look at some of the fundamental ratios in each of the categories, starting with the profitability category.

In the *profitability* category there are at least three general purpose ratios that are capable of being calculated for every organization. The key ratio is one that helps us understand whether we are able to generate an adequate return on our investment in resources. This ratio is called the return on capital employed. From the owners' perspectives, we are also interested in the return on ordinary shareholders' funds. These two ratios use a different calculation of profit as their numerator. For return on capital employed we use operating profit less and income tax applicable to that. The reason for this is that the ratio looks to measure the returns to all investors before any distributions are made to them. As far as the owners are concerned, we use the net profit attributable to ordinary shareholders as the numerator in our ratio. The third general purpose ratio in this category is operating profit margin. The operating profit, that is, profit before interest and taxation, is used in this ratio as it represents the profit from trading operations. We shall compare it with our sales revenue to understand more about the profitability of our relationships with customers.

In the *asset management effectiveness* category there are also three general purpose ratios that are used. They each represent a number of days and relate to the time it takes to sell inventory, how long it takes our customers to pay us, and how long it is before we pay our suppliers. Each of these is an important factor in our organization's cash flow. When we add them together, we understand how many days it takes us to circulate one dollar through our organization. This is known as the working capital cycle, and it is calculated thus:

Inventory turnover + days' sales outstanding – days' payables outstanding

In the *liquidity* category there are two key ratios that are intended to indicate whether we can meet our obligations and when they fall due. The first, the current ratio, simply compares current assets with current liabilities. The higher the ratio, the more liquid our organization is considered to be. This is, unfortunately, not always the case as the numerator, current assets, includes the book value of our inventories, and these cannot be converted into cash quickly. We need an alternative measure, a more stringent measure. This is the acid test ratio, which is the second ratio in this category. It is similar to the current ratio in all respects except that inventories are excluded from the current assets.

In the *financial leverage* category we are principally interested in only one ratio and that is the one that measures the contribution of long-term lenders to the capital structure of our organization. If the result of this calculation indicates an unacceptably high proportion of debt finance then we would probably check the interest cover ratio as well. This looks at how many times our operating profit will cover the amount of interest payable. Together they help us understand the risk to lenders that we shall not be able to meet our commitments to them as well the risk to the owners that the lenders will take action to recover monies due to them.

The final category of ratios is the *investment* ratios, and these relate principally to the owners. These ratios are designed to help equity investors assess the returns on their investment. They include the dividend payout ratio, the dividend yield ratio, the earnings per share ratio, and the price/earnings ratio. Only two of these, the dividend payout ratio and the earnings per share ratio, are applicable to every company. The other two require market-based information that is usually only available for companies listed on a stock exchange.

As is usually the case with information derived from accounting data, there are some limitations to ratio analysis—the most important of which is that ratios are only as reliable as the financial statements from which they derive. What is more, the snapshot nature of the statement of financial position, which provides the data for a number of ratios, means that the calculation could provide misleading information if, as is frequently the case, assets and liabilities are actively managed to present the best possible view on the balance date.

To finish this all-too-brief discussion, please remember this: No ratio has a single correct value. Like Goldilocks and the three bears, the observation that the value of a ratio is too high, too low, or just right depends on the perspective of the analyst and on our competitive strategy. It is the interpretation and presentation of the significant results and trends indicated by our calculations that is of greater value.

Trend Analysis

It is often helpful to see whether ratios are indicating trends. Rather than simply looking at a table of numbers, we can plot key ratios on a graph to provide a simple visual display of changes occurring over time in our own performance as well as a comparison with our rivals or the industry as a whole. Figure 8.1 provides an illustration of trend analysis.

Figure 8.1. Trend analysis.

Benchmarking

Benchmarking is a process where we identify best practice in relation to the performance characteristics of our products or services and the processes by which they are created and delivered. Our search for best practice can take place both inside our industry and in other industries where we look for any lessons that we can learn. The objective of benchmarking is to understand and evaluate our current position in relation to best practice and to identify areas and means of improving our performance.

Benchmarking involves looking outward, that is, outside our organization, industry, region, or country, to understand how others achieve their performance levels and to understand the processes they use. In this way benchmarking helps to explain excellent performance. When we apply the lessons learned from a benchmarking exercise, we expect to see improved performance in critical functions within our organization or in our relationships with other stakeholders.

Think!
How frequently do you benchmark performance against your competitors? Are you happy to be better than average? What is your target?

The process of benchmarking should never be considered a one-off exercise. For it to be effective, it must be ongoing and lie at the heart of monitoring our performance with the idea that we should never lose sight of ever-improving best practice.

Case Study

Analyzing Performance at Bull-Roo Enterprises Limited

When the company was just starting out, analyzing performance was a difficult thing to do. With no history to compare against and no real competitors to speak of, unless you considered the mighty *sogo shosha* competitors, the only comparisons that could be drawn were with the plans and targets that were developed.

As time went by and a history was established, it became possible to analyze trends in performance. There were only a few ratios that interested Pearl and her team, and they related to profitability and asset management effectiveness. They were keen to understand how their return on capital employed tracked over the years as well as their ability to add value, considering added value as a proportion of sales as their yardstick. Because of the factoring arrangements Keith negotiated in the early days of the company, an arrangement that continues, there was little concern about receivables. Payables had never been an issue as they adhered to agreed payment arrangements to the letter. So from an effective asset management perspective, their only area of concern was inventory and how long it remained in their warehouse.

After showing steady growth for a number of years, the company's return on capital employed had leveled off and, indeed, in the last couple of years had shown a downward trend. At the same time they were holding progressively more inventory, which was not really what they had in mind when they first started out. They would take commissions to source supplies for the wine industry and purchasers for their product. In recent years Doug had taken to overordering on the basis that he would always find a buyer, but the economic situation was beginning to deteriorate and some lines in inventory were becoming a millstone. They needed to do something about this, and soon. On the upside, they continued to steadily increase their value added thanks in no small part to the excellent reputation they had built. The excess inventory certainly helped on that front, so perhaps it wasn't such a bad thing after all.

Summary

The interpretation of any ratio depends on the industry. In particular the ratio needs to be interpreted as a trend over time or by comparison to industry averages or to competitor ratios or to predetermined targets. These comparisons help determine whether performance is improving and where further improvement may be necessary. Based on an understanding of the business context and competitive conditions, and the information provided by ratio analysis, we can make judgments about the pattern of past performance, prospects for an organization, and its financial strength.

This form of analysis, however, does not provide all the solutions. It is, at best, a means to an end. It simply helps in our overall analysis and questioning. Financial statements not only change according to fundamental rules but also are affected by emotion, economic cycles, and many other factors. That said, there are few institutions, banks, or investors that will make a decision without a full and complete ratio analysis to support their judgment.

PART V

Where to Next?

We are nearing the end of our story. In looking at this important discipline of financial management we have traveled a long road by identifying where we are, working out where we want to be, deciding on the best way to get there, and then looking to see if we actually made it. This happens continuously throughout the life of our organization in cycles of varying duration. The last question we must ask ourselves is this: Having experienced this journey and having reached our destination for this cycle, where do we want to go next?

To help us make that decision we need to understand whether it was all worthwhile. Did we really create something of value? How can we find the answer to that question? In this section we'll look at several ways of doing this, so that, like Marco Polo on his travels along the Silk Road, we will be better able to understand whether we are improving our lot every time we make a change in our strategic direction.

What, in reality, is value creation? Figure 9.1 shows us how this works when we play chess. There we create value by successfully getting a pawn

Figure 9.1. Creating value.

to the opposite end of the board and converting it into a queen. In business it is not that easy to recognize. We can surely play with some models that will help us understand, theoretically, if we have created value, but in the end it will only be realized if someone else is prepared to buy our creation. Until then, for us value is but a dream. To paraphrase an old saying, *value is in the eye of the beholder.*

And so it is when it comes to a merger or an acquisition. Any value we calculate using one of the readily available models can only ever be used to provide the boundaries for negotiation. Like any commercial transaction between two parties, the final price will inevitably be shaped by a number of nonfinancial factors, including the negotiating skills and the relative bargaining position of the parties.

CHAPTER 9

Are We Creating Value for Owners?

Introduction

How do we know if we, as managers, are really creating value for our owners? It is questionable whether anyone has a precise definition of what wealth maximization means to owners, let alone other investors. Is it a dividend stream, future earnings, or some combination of the two that incorporates capital gains? Do we take a decision to retain earnings for reinvestment and go for growth, or do we distribute profit to owners? It is doubtful that the choice we make will satisfy every owner's expectation.

Of greater concern is that our perception of income may differ from investors' perceptions not simply because we have access to more detailed data or that we employ different valuation models but because our behavior is often motivated by personal greed rather than owner welfare. Such behavior has the potential to lead to irrational decisions and financial panic as we saw in 2008. From the outside looking in, is there a way of using published financial data to measure the consequences of our strategic decisions?

New Forms of Measurement

Traditional accounting-based measures of management effectiveness, like the return on capital employed ratio and the earnings per share value, have been criticized for not focusing sufficiently on what businesses ultimately seek to do: to generate wealth or value for their owners.

> ***Think!***
> How do you know whether you are creating value for the owners of your organization?

The problem with accounting measures is that they tend to focus on sales and profit increases, not on value generation. For example, it is always open to a business to increase its return on capital employed and earnings per share, at least in the short term, by taking on more risky activities. Such activities may well have the effect of reducing owner value. The increasing emphasis on the wealth of owners as a corporate objective has led to the emergence of ideas like shareholder value analysis and economic value added (EVA).

Shareholder Value Analysis

Shareholder value analysis is based on the totally logical principle that the value of the organization is equal to the sum of the net present values of all its activities. This is to say that, at any point in time, our organization has a value equal to the projected future cash flows from all its existing projects, discounted at a suitable rate. The owners' financial stake in the organization is its full value less any outstanding debt. Hence if the sum of the net present values of our various activities can be increased then this should mean greater value for owners either to be paid out as dividends or reinvested in other projects that will, in turn, result in still more value for owners.

Adopting shareholder value analysis indicates a commitment to managing our organization in a way that maximizes returns to owners. As such, it becomes a powerful tool for strategic planning purposes. For example, because it takes account of all the elements that determine owner value, it is extremely useful when considering major shifts of direction such as these:

- acquiring new businesses
- selling existing businesses
- developing new products or markets
- reorganizing or restructuring our organization

Probably, the most helpful contribution shareholder value analysis can provide to managing an organization is that it highlights the key drivers of value. This enables us to set targets for achieving value-enhancing strategies in each area. It can help create an environment where value enhancement is on top of the agenda for everyone in the organization. In this way, the organization's primary financial objective is linked directly to its day-to-day decisions and actions.

There are constructive arguments to suggest that shareholder value analysis should replace the traditional accounting measures of value creation, such as profit, return on capital employed, and earnings per share. One thing is for sure: Shareholder value analysis is a radical departure from convention. It requires different performance indicators, different reporting systems, and different management methods. Indeed, it may also require a change in culture within our organization to promote the emphasis on maximization of owner wealth.

Economic Value Added

The use of economic profit as a performance indicator reflects the notion that, for an organization to be profitable in an economic sense, it must generate returns that exceed those required by investors. It is not enough simply to make an accounting profit because this in no way represents required investor returns. The economic profit approach has a long history and is widely used. Economic value added, or EVA, is a refinement of the economic profit approach that was developed and trademarked by the New York management consultancy firm Stern Stewart and Company.

EVA is a measure of the extent to which, if at all, our after-tax operating profit for the period exceeds the required minimum profit, which in turn is based on the investors' minimum required rate of return—their weighted average cost of capital (WACC)—on their investment multiplied by that investment. The formula is

EVA = net operating profit after tax − (WACC × capital invested).

If there is an excess of actual profit over the required minimum, then economic value will have been added and the owners will be wealthier. If there is a shortfall, then the owners will be less wealthy because they will not have earned the return they expected, given the amount of investment and the required rate of return. The value of our organization is the present value of expected EVA plus the capital invested.

EVA relies on conventional financial statements to measure the wealth created for owners. Unfortunately, because of the problems

Think!
Look back over the last few years. Try using one of these models to see if your organization has been creating value for its owners.

and limitations of conventional measures, the figures for net operating profit after tax and capital invested have to be adjusted. To give you an idea, profit is probably understated because of the arbitrary write-offs associated with internal investment in intangible assets. Capital is also likely to be understated because assets are recorded at their unallocated original cost, which can produce figures considerably below current market values.

Stern Stewart has identified more than 100 adjustments that ought to be made to the conventional financial statements; however, only a handful are probably needed to produce a reliable measurement. Unless an adjustment is going to have a significant effect on the calculation, it really is not worth making. Whichever adjustments are made, they should reflect the nature of our activities. Put more simply, every organization is unique and so we must customize the calculation of EVA to our particular circumstances.

Market Value Added

EVA is really designed for internal management purposes. Its developers produced another measure to complement EVA and to provide owners with a way of tracking changes in shareholder value over time. Market value added measures the gains or losses in shareholder value by measuring the difference between the market value of the organization and the total value of the investment that has been made in it over the years. The market value of our organization is usually taken to be the market value of both the equity and loan capital. The total investment comprises the book values of loan capital, share capital, and retained earnings.

We can see that market value added is actually a very simple idea, but it has one important drawback. If shares are not listed on a stock exchange then we can't determine a market value of equity, and as a result it is not really possible to measure market value added. If we can use this model, then we simply compare the cash value of the investment with the cash invested. If the cash value is more then there has been an increase in owner value, and if it is less then owner value has been destroyed.

Apart from the drawback already mentioned, market value added has other limitations in that it can only be applied to assess an organization as a whole, as there are no separate market prices available for strategic business units.

Links

Although at first glance it may appear that shareholder value analysis and economic value added are worlds apart, this is not the case. In fact, the opposite is true. They are closely related, so close in fact that they should both produce the same figure for owner value. Although both are consistent with the objective of maximizing the wealth of owners, it is claimed that EVA has a number of practical advantages over shareholder value analysis. The most obvious is that EVA is more closely related to conventional financial reporting systems and financial reports and, therefore, unlike shareholder value analysis, does not require the development of entirely new systems.

There is a strong relationship between EVA and market value added. We saw earlier that the value of our organization is equal to the present value (PV) of future expected EVA plus the capital invested. If we put this another way, then we find that

$$\text{PV of future EVA} = \text{organization value} - \text{capital invested.}$$

Similarly, market value added is the difference between organizational value and the capital invested, and so we are able to draw each of the three models together as they should, in theory, all produce the same figure for organizational value.

Case Study

Value Creation at Bull-Roo Enterprises Limited

Pearl has been living her dream. She and her team have been moderately successful in that they have earned a good living, made some wonderful friends along the way, and have created a reputable and financially sound organization. What is more, they managed to achieve the majority of targets they set for each of the journeys on which they embarked. You really couldn't ask for more than that, now could you?

They now need to understand just how much value they have created and so have to make a choice between the available models. Having remained a private organization there is nothing readily available that will give them an indication of their market value. What they do have is a detailed analysis of their future expectations, which includes cash flow projections.

Pearl decides to use this information in the shareholder value analysis model to help her better understand the value of Bull-Roo Enterprises Limited. EVA is a little too complex for her, and she doesn't want to ask Keith to help as he will only want to know why she needs the information. In truth she is getting tired. The business has kept her very busy for a number of years, and she would really like to spend more time with her family. She completes her calculations and is pleasantly surprised. The real question is whether someone else sees the same value in her company. Christmas is coming. Perhaps this is something best left until the New Year.

Summary

I have introduced three models that can be used for understanding the value of an organization to its owners. Each of them is calculated in a different way, but as you would probably expect, they should each produce the same outcome. Our choice of model may well be determined by the data we have available. Nevertheless, we need to undertake a periodic assessment of whether value has been created for the owners. One of these models, perhaps a different one at different times, will serve us well in that regard.

CHAPTER 10

Business Mergers and Valuation

A merger is one way we are able to enhance organizational sustainability by expanding operations. Mergers occur when the merging organizations have a mutual interest in joining forces. This is decidedly different from an acquisition, which is a predatory move by one organization on another and is often not welcome resulting in a hostile takeover. Which of these it is may be different in the minds of the parties to the transaction as depicted in Figure 10.1. Mergers and acquisitions of other companies are investment decisions and should be evaluated on essentially the same basis as, say, the purchase of new items of machinery. There are, however, two important differences between this type of activity and many standard investments.

Figure 10.1. Thinking about mergers and acquisitions.

First, because acquisitions are frequently resisted by the target's managers, instigators often have little or no intelligence about their targets beyond published financial and market data and any inside information they may obtain. Once they have declared their position, the situation changes. When the bid process is underway, the defending board is obliged to provide key information to enable the instigator to conduct *due diligence* examinations, which are essentially searches for skeletons in the cupboard.

Second, many acquisitions are undertaken for long-term strategic motives, and the benefits are often difficult to quantify. It is not unusual to hear the chairman of the predator talking about an acquisition opening up a strategic window. What they often do not add is that the window not only is usually shut but also has thick curtains drawn across it. To a large extent an acquisition is a shot in the dark, which partly explains why so many organizations that proceed with one suffer greatly afterward. Of course, this is not the only reason for failure. On occasion a target is simply too large in relation to the instigator, so excessive borrowings or unexpected integration problems strangle the parent.

Given that acquisitions have uncertain outcomes, the larger they are the more catastrophic the impact of any adverse events. As a result, it may be more rational and less risky to confine activity to small, uncontested bids. Alternatively, a spread of large acquisitions might confer significant portfolio diversification benefits. The greater the scale of takeover activity, however, the greater the resulting financing burden placed on the instigator and the greater the impact of diverting managerial capacity into solving integration problems.

Clearly, another critical element of mergers and acquisitions is the proposed financing method. Cash has been, and continues to be, a popular medium for financing acquisitions. There was a time, however, when more emphasis was placed on the use of debt as the primary means of such financing. The use of debt to finance acquisitions has declined dramatically with the higher valuations of target enterprises. As a result, shares in the instigator are now routinely used to finance acquisitions. Of course, the total financing package could comprise elements of each of these options. Several considerations guide the selection of the medium of exchange. Among the most important are tax considerations, accounting treatment, managerial control issues, financial returns to owners, and the existence of slack, which is defined as unused financial resources.

Without a doubt, the acquisition decision is a complex one. It involves significant uncertainties, often requires substantial funding, and may pose awkward problems of integration. Yet as some acquisition kings have shown, spectacular payoffs can be achieved.

Why Do Mergers Occur?

Throughout the book I have tried to emphasize that, for virtually every organization other than a not-for-profit or government authority, the major objective must be to maximize value for the current owners. This is absolutely necessary for any one of a number of reasons that include borrowing to diversify, looking to sell the organization, privatizing of public sector entities, or converting from a private to a public organization.

The best way for us to maximize value is to actively manage our resource, liability, and equity bases because if we don't then somebody else will. Our organization may well be absorbed by another because they believe they will be able to better maximize value for owners. This is the first, and principal, reason for merger and acquisition activity.

There are other reasons for engaging this activity, probably the most common of which is the belief that synergies exist allowing the two organizations to work more efficiently together than either would separately. Such synergies usually result from their combined ability to exploit economies of scale, eliminate duplication in many functional areas, share managerial expertise, and raise larger amounts of capital. If successful, then this is an excellent way of increasing owners' wealth.

Mergers between organizations operating in the same industry are often motivated by a desire for greater market share. In some cases, tax advantages may be derived from a merger or acquisition, but this is rarely a key consideration in prompting organizations to merge. More often merger or acquisition activity is part of a deliberate strategy of diversification, allowing the predator, or the combined organization, to exploit new markets and spread its risk.

On the other hand, we may instigate an acquisition because we think the target is undervalued. This means that we have found a *bargain*—a good investment capable of generating an abnormally high return for our

Think!
Why did AOL merge with Time Warner? Would AOL have survived the dot-com crash if it hadn't?

owners. Unfortunately, there are also times when acquisitions are simply motivated by the management team's desire to *empire build*. Rarely are these acquisitions successful in anything other than promoting certain individuals' super-egos and boosting their pay packets.

Finally, the owners of an organization may seek a merger or an acquisition when they no longer wish to operate the enterprise themselves. Perhaps in these cases it would be simpler to sell their share of the organization to someone else, but this is likely to result only in a change of ownership without accruing any of the benefits associated with joining forces with another organization.

Who Benefits?

The principal benefit from a merger or an acquisition arises from increased cost efficiency and an increase in market share, which often leads to an increase in value generation. If this is the case, and really it shouldn't be any other way, then our owners' wealth after a merger or acquisition should be greater than the sum of the owners' wealth in each of the participating organizations. Of course, it doesn't always work out that way, and there are many examples to show that. Shaun Rein[1] suggests that in 70% of merger and acquisition cases the owners would have been better off not getting involved at all.

Any discussion concerning winners and losers in merger and acquisition activity must include the management teams of both the bidding and target organizations. They are important stakeholders in their respective organizations and play a significant role in negotiations. In the case of an acquisition, the management team of the predator will often benefit considerably in that they will manage an enlarged organization, which will, in turn, result in greater status, income, and security. For their counterparts in the acquired organization, the situation is less certain, with some being retained but others being demoted or shown the door. Something similar happens in the case of mergers as the combined organization seeks to exploit synergies from the merger.

Think!
Have you ever been involved in a merger or acquisition? How tough was it? Were there really any benefits? If so, who got them?

It will come as no surprise to many readers that mergers and acquisitions can be very rewarding for the investment advisers and lawyers engaged by each organization. They will receive fees for providing advice and putting together the financing package. In many cases the advisers acting for the target, in the case of an acquisition, receive higher fees to compensate them for the loss of a client.

What Makes a Successful Merger?

Earlier I suggested that in the majority of merger and acquisition cases the owners would have been better off not proceeding. Obviously, there are times where success is achieved. What are the magic ingredients of success? It is generally accepted that there are several factors consistently present in successful mergers and acquisitions, which relate to *strategy*, *fit*, *integration*, *motive*, *price*, and *ownership*.

A merger or acquisition intended to achieve our *strategy* is the only basis on which we should proceed. If we can't explain how the deal will help us reach the destination on our long road then it shouldn't be done. There are quite a few strategic reasons to engage in a merger or acquisition, but the best ones relate to getting our hands on complementary product lines, securing innovative technical skills, accessing new markets and customers, and leveraging existing resources. Just because an organization is available and we can afford it are not good enough reasons to get involved.

Fit, which is another way of describing organizational culture, considers such things as whether the deal will be acceptable to employees of both organizations, whether the new management team is able to speak with one voice, or whether any customers will be alienated by existing reputations. It certainly is an intangible, but nevertheless critical, factor in the success of a merger or an acquisition. It's unlikely that any deal will provide a perfect fit, so it is essential that both organizations assess these cultural issues in advance and identify the worst-case scenario. If we decide that losing some good people and potentially some customers is bad for the future then we should reconsider our plans.

Successful *integration* of the two organizations will have an enormous impact on the success of the merger or acquisition. Understanding what will be necessary to achieve a successful integration needs to start at the time a merger or an acquisition is being considered because integration costs have to be taken into consideration when determining the price.

With a merger or acquisition it's important to understand what each party's *motive* is for entering the transaction. If the organization has been offered for sale and you are thinking of buying, then never assume you know the reason why it is being sold. Always ask why, and be skeptical about the answer. There could be a really valid reason, but if there is so much opportunity, why are they selling? What do they know about their organization and its future that they are not telling you? What about you? What are your reasons for thinking about acquiring or merging with that particular organization? Maybe it has something special, such as a strong customer base, a leading-edge product, or a well-known brand name, that will allow you to grow your organization faster than building it up internally. Or maybe you just want to stroke your ego and increase your pay packet by managing a bigger organization. Whatever the motives on either side, understanding them up front will help you structure the right deal for everyone.

The *price* is always important. Remember, as with any other investment, you must be able to generate a return greater than the cost of financing your organization. The higher the price the greater the returns, in absolute terms, that you need to get from the investment and the smaller cushion you have for unexpected problems. On the other hand, securing a low price does not always equate to a good deal and may be a good indicator that all is not as it seems. In any merger or acquisition there is a pricing range based on different assumptions of future performance. In the case of an acquisition, the predator has to decide what price to offer in that range or how the risk will be divided between the respective owners. In a competitive, strategic situation it is often the case that predators will be forced to pay more than they would like, although they should always know the maximum they are willing to pay and not exceed it even if it means losing the opportunity.

Once the merger or acquisition transaction has been completed, someone, preferably a highly respected individual who was closely associated with the negotiations, needs to take *ownership* of the new organization. This person needs to be its champion and not simply view the acquisition or merged organization as another project to be delegated. Melding the two organizations is never going to be an easy task, and so while everyone on the integration team needs to focus on the important issues, this one person needs to be given some specific targets and held personally accountable for achieving them.

Valuing a Business

An important aspect of any merger or acquisition negotiation is the value to be placed on the organization to be merged or acquired. There are several methods that can be used to derive an appropriate value of an organization, which are not, of course, used only in the context of merger or acquisition negotiations. They will also be required in other circumstances, although they remain a vital element in this activity.

In theory, the value of an organization may be defined in terms of either the current value of the resources it controls or the future cash flows generated from those resources. In a world of perfect information and perfect certainty, valuing an organization would pose few problems. In the real world, however, measurement and forecasting problems conspire to make the valuation process difficult. Various valuation methods have been developed to deal with these problems, but they often produce quite different results.

The main methods employed to value organizations fall into one of three broad categories. These are methods that are based on the value of an organization's resources, use stock market information, or predict future cash flows.

Resource-based methods attempt to value an organization by reference to the resources it controls. The simplest way is to use the resources statement that is published by the organization. It will show a value for resources as well as the amount of external claims against those resources, or liabilities. By subtracting the claims from the value of resources we can arrive at one value for the organization. Using this method has the advantage that the valuation process is straightforward and the data are easy to obtain.

The value of an organization obtained in this way, however, is likely to be extremely conservative. This is because a number of resources that the organization controls, such as brand names, internally generated goodwill, and intellectual capital, may not be shown on the resources statement and will be ignored for the purposes of valuation. What is more, many of the items are often shown at their historic cost, which may be well below their current market value. We can try to overcome this particular flaw by using current market values rather than the values shown on the resources statement. These could be based on either net realizable value or replacement cost. In practice, a combination of both valuation approaches may be used.

Use of stock market information is only directly relevant to a company whose shares are listed on one of the many stock exchanges around the world. Since it is generally accepted that share prices react quickly, and in an unbiased manner, to new information that becomes publicly available, the value of a listed company is easily determined. This, of course, doesn't help when we are looking at other organizations. It doesn't stop us, however, from using stock market information and ratios to help value an unlisted organization.

The first step is to find a listed company within the same industry that has similar risk and growth characteristics. Stock market ratios relating to the listed company can then be applied to the unlisted organization to approximate its value. The key ratio here is the price to earnings ratio. By simply multiplying the unlisted organization's earnings by the price to earnings ratio of the listed company we can arrive at an approximate market value for the unlisted organization.

We have already seen that the value of a resource is equivalent to the present value of the cash flow it generates. There are two methods we can use here. The first, the *dividend valuation method*, was first introduced in chapter 5. This method works on the basis that the valuation of an organization is based on its current dividend, the expected future growth rate of that dividend, and the required rate of return on equity capital. While this method is intuitively appealing, there are practical problems in forecasting future dividend payments and in calculating the required rate of return. On top of this, the use of dividends as a basis for valuation poses a problem because of their discretionary nature. Different organizations will adopt different payout policies thereby affecting valuation calculations. Nowhere is this more evident than in the case of high-growth organizations that choose to plow profit back into their organization rather than make dividend payments.

The second, the *free cash flow method*, determines an organization's value by reference to the free cash flow that it generates over a period of time. Free cash flows are those available to investors after any new investments in resources. In other words, they are equivalent to the cash flow from operations after deducting income taxes paid and cash for investment. The valuation process is the same as we have used previously, and that is to discount the future free cash flows over time using the weighted average cost of capital. The present value of these future cash flows, less amounts owing to long-term lenders at current market values, will represent the value of the organization. The major problem with this method is that of accurate forecasting—an endemic problem in every aspect of business life when trying to understand the future.

There are other methods available to us, some of which, such as shareholder value analysis and economic value added, we looked at in some detail in chapter 9. Using any of these methods to value a well-established organization is not without problems, but those problems will appear trivial when struggling with the difficulties of valuing newly established organizations. These organizations have no track record and may be making little or no profit, rendering any of these valuation models impotent. In these situations one way of calculating an organization's value is to apply an industry multiplier to the gross sales or the gross profit of the organization. The drawback here is that industry multipliers generally represent the industry average, and very few organizations operate at or around, averages, which would overvalue or undervalue an organization if such a rule of thumb is applied. All the same, at least our estimation will serve a purpose, even if that is simply to provide a starting point for negotiations.

Choosing a Valuation Model

When deciding on the valuation model to employ we need to consider the underlying purpose of the merger or acquisition. Different valuation models may be appropriate for different circumstances. Let me give you an example. If the predator is looking to acquire an organization simply to break it up and sell it piece by piece, then it would probably be most interested in the liquidation basis of valuation. On the other hand, where market prices are available these will be used as a basis for negotiation.

Think!
As you can see, valuation is not an easy task. Why don't you try, using one of the ways suggested here, to value your organization? Ask a colleague to do the same, and then compare the results. How close are you?

In every situation, whichever method is used to value an organization, the result is only going to provide an approximation that will help set the boundaries within which a final price will be determined. This final price will, however, be influenced by various factors, including the negotiating skills and the relative bargaining position of the parties.

Case Study

The Acquisition of Bull-Roo Enterprises Limited

Christmas has come and gone, and now it's time for Pearl to make the decision that will affect the rest of her life. She has enjoyed the experience of running her own business, but she feels that her time has come and she should allow someone else to take over the company and continue to drive it forward. Her decision made, she now faces the unenviable task of telling her two colleagues, Keith and Doug, who have given so much of their time, effort, and financial support into making Bull-Roo Enterprises Limited such a successful venture. Another Sunday lunch is necessary!

Together they enjoy their lunch, although both Keith and Doug know that something is in the wind. After lunch and over coffee, Pearl finally tells them what she has in mind. For Keith it is not a surprise, but Doug takes the news badly. He has developed into a first-class manager and, in more recent times, has become the driving force behind many of the forward-looking developments in the company. Keith, on the other hand, welcomes Pearl's decision as it will finally give him the chance to retire and enjoy life at a slower pace.

The next day Doug stopped by Pearl's office for a chat. He asked Keith to come along, as what he had to say was important to the three of them. The previous evening, troubled by the possibility that he would not be able to continue with the venture that provided vitality in his life, he had a long conversation with an old classmate from his MBA days. Caroline had carved out a successful career for herself as a stockbroker and was looking for something new and adventurous to occupy her life. Doug sang the praises of Bull-Roo Enterprises Limited to her and asked, point blank, if she would be interested in joining him in making a bid for the company. He had no idea how much it would cost, but he did have one advantage. Over the years, with Pearl's blessing, he had built up his ownership stake slowly but surely to the point where he now held 18% of the equity. More than a little excited at the prospect, Caroline agreed to look into this some more. Now Doug was asking Pearl for permission to formally conduct due diligence; although, having been at the heart of the organization for some time, he had a better idea of the situation than most. Caroline, on the other hand, needed the assurance.

Keith nodded his assent, and Pearl happily gave Caroline and Doug permission to proceed. She was confident they would find everything OK and a reasonable price would be offered for the company. It had been a wonderful journey. Together they had achieved much, and she was sure their spirit would live on in the company under new ownership.

Summary

Mergers or acquisitions have a particular place in the commercial world's circle of life. As I have tried to show with my little case study, business enterprise is a journey—a journey that is dreamed about, planned, carried out, and ultimately finished when the destination is reached. These journeys can be quite short, exceptionally long, or a collection of mixed-length journeys. Each journey in a collection represents an individual circle in the life of an organization. Even those organizations that have existed since what seems to be time immemorial, such as the remarkable *ryokan*—Hotel Sakan in Sendai, Japan—that has been in existence for more than 1,000 years and, I believe, operated by the same family for more than 25 generations, have been through a succession of these circles as they reach one destination and then start out in search of another.

When a destination is reached, or even just before we get there, we need to think about whether we wish to continue our journey to another place. If we do, then it is simply a matter of starting a new circle in the life of the organization. If we don't, then we either bring the life of our organization to a close or find someone else who is interested in taking it on its new journey—its next circle of life. This is the role played by merger and acquisition activity.

There is a lot to consider when we are thinking of acquiring or merging with another organization, but nothing is more important than deciding on the price we want to pay. If we don't get somewhere near the mark with our offer, then the impact on our own existence could be terminal. Determining the amount to pay, in other words valuing the organization, is such a subjective task. However we decide to calculate this amount, it will not be precise but simply an approximation that will allow us to start negotiating.

With any merger or acquisition, understanding what we are getting is the first important step, knowing how much to pay is the second important step, and integrating the two organizations is the third important step. In the end, is it worth the effort? This depends entirely on what is being bought. There are unique merger or acquisition opportunities that can dramatically improve our position in our market, or provide access to new markets. With careful planning, analysis, and hard work by the management team, mergers or acquisitions can be an excellent way to help us reach our destination in this particular circle of life.

Epilogue

The economic realities of the last few years since 2007 have brought into focus the importance of our ability to adapt quickly to change. Unfortunately, most of the change we have seen has been to adopt a short-term survival mode—one in which cost-cutting measures have priority over long-term planning. This reflects 20th-century management at its worst, showing little or no acceptance of ideas, concepts, and thinking that might be used to improve practice in the quest for a sustainable competitive advantage. In the face of economic disruption many of us are quite obviously not prepared to refine our beliefs about how things could be better done.

Unfortunately, experience shows us that refining beliefs is not quite as easy as it sounds. Human beings become very comfortable with the particular set of beliefs that have gotten them where they are. In other words, they become much attached to the ideas that have served them so well in the past. It is only a preparedness to ask the really difficult questions that allows us to confront the possibility that those ideas typically have a use-by date. After all, no system, no framework, no model, however effective, will remain current indefinitely. And so it will be with everything that I've discussed in this book. We must not allow the certain truths of today to become the unquestioned myths of tomorrow.

I'm convinced that the thoughts and ideas I've put forward in this book provide ample fuel to critically challenge some of the currently prevailing myths that underpin financial management in our organizations today. I sincerely hope they will lead to a meaningful change in the way we understand the life of our organization, the journey it takes from concept to conclusion, and the things we do to ensure the smoothest and most comfortable ride possible. Only we can bring about this change, and for many of us this will mean a complete transformation in the way we think, which will only ever be achieved through a process of learning.

For nearly 200 years, management, and financial management in particular, has been dominated by financial reflections on the past. This is probably because we neither had the power nor the tools to demonstrate the future impact in a manner acceptable in a traditional organizational culture—a culture constrained by autocratic management and infused with a short-term financial focus dominated by the *bottom line*. This culture led to the involuntary adoption by many of what has become known as the McNamara[1] fallacy:

> The first step is to measure whatever can be easily measured. This is OK as far as it goes. The second step is to disregard that which can't be easily measured or to give it an arbitrary quantitative value. This is artificial and misleading. The third step is to presume that what can't be measured easily really isn't important. This is blindness. The fourth step is to say that what can't be easily measured really doesn't exist. This is suicide.

We can't change the past, only learn from it, and so we shouldn't spend so much time worrying about it. Remember, history is the prologue to the future. There are kings (board of directors) and there are prophets (finance managers). The kings have the power, and the prophets have the principles. Kings are the people who make things happen, but all kings, and increasingly queens, need a prophet to keep them informed amidst the confusion of change. Prophets, in spite of their name, do not foretell the future. What they can, and must, do is tell the truth as they see it. They can advise about the road ahead. They can advise about things they believe are wrong, unjust, or prejudiced. Most of all, they can clarify uncertainties and bring focus to the issues.[2]

So you can see, we will be better served by devoting our time and thought into looking at how we may incorporate the impact of forward thinking into the tools we use to manage our organizations. This will take time, for change does not happen overnight. Even Royal Dutch Shell plc, with all the resources at its disposal, recognizes that introducing fundamental changes to conventional wisdom may take many years and that it is often a long and tortuous process.

The aim of this book was to provide, which I trust I have done, some ideas and concepts to act as signposts on our organization's road map. Of course, nothing may ever be considered all encompassing. What I have included in this book was never expected to be so. It was only intended to act as a catalyst for thinking about a more comprehensive way of ensuring our organization reaches its destination safely and successfully.

We have now come to the end of this book. I hope you have enjoyed reading it and that, in some way, it will provide you with some good ideas for your organization. But to quote a statesman[3] from an earlier era, "Now this is not the end. It is not even the beginning of the end. But it is, perhaps, the end of the beginning."

Thank you so much!

Appendix

Present Value (1 + i) – n

Year	1%	2%	3%	4%	5%	6%	7%	8%	9%	10%
1	0.990	0.980	0.971	0.962	0.952	0.943	0.935	0.926	0.917	0.909
2	0.980	0.961	0.943	0.925	0.907	0.890	0.873	0.857	0.842	0.826
3	0.971	0.942	0.915	0.889	0.864	0.840	0.816	0.794	0.772	0.751
4	0.961	0.924	0.888	0.855	0.823	0.792	0.763	0.735	0.708	0.683
5	0.951	0.906	0.863	0.822	0.784	0.747	0.713	0.681	0.650	0.621
6	0.942	0.888	0.837	0.790	0.746	0.705	0.666	0.630	0.596	0.564
7	0.933	0.871	0.813	0.760	0.711	0.665	0.623	0.583	0.547	0.513
8	0.923	0.853	0.789	0.731	0.677	0.627	0.582	0.540	0.502	0.467
9	0.914	0.837	0.766	0.703	0.645	0.592	0.544	0.500	0.460	0.424
10	0.905	0.820	0.744	0.676	0.614	0.558	0.508	0.463	0.422	0.386
Year	**11%**	**12%**	**13%**	**14%**	**15%**	**16%**	**17%**	**18%**	**19%**	**20%**
1	0.901	0.893	0.885	0.877	0.870	0.862	0.855	0.847	0.840	0.833
2	0.812	0.797	0.783	0.769	0.756	0.743	0.731	0.718	0.706	0.694
3	0.731	0.712	0.693	0.675	0.658	0.641	0.624	0.609	0.593	0.579
4	0.659	0.636	0.613	0.592	0.572	0.552	0.534	0.516	0.499	0.482
5	0.593	0.567	0.543	0.519	0.497	0.476	0.456	0.437	0.419	0.402
6	0.535	0.507	0.480	0.456	0.432	0.410	0.390	0.370	0.352	0.335
7	0.482	0.452	0.425	0.400	0.376	0.354	0.333	0.314	0.296	0.279
8	0.434	0.404	0.376	0.351	0.327	0.305	0.285	0.266	0.249	0.233
9	0.391	0.361	0.333	0.308	0.284	0.263	0.243	0.226	0.209	0.194
10	0.352	0.322	0.295	0.270	0.247	0.227	0.208	0.191	0.176	0.162

Annuity [1 – (1+ i) – n] / i

Year	1%	2%	3%	4%	5%	6%	7%	8%	9%	10%
1	0.990	0.980	0.971	0.962	0.952	0.943	0.935	0.926	0.917	0.909
2	1.970	1.942	1.913	1.886	1.859	1.833	1.808	1.783	1.759	1.736
3	2.941	2.884	2.829	2.775	2.723	2.673	2.624	2.577	2.531	2.487
4	3.902	3.808	3.717	3.630	3.546	3.465	3.387	3.312	3.240	3.170
5	4.853	4.713	4.580	4.452	4.329	4.212	4.100	3.993	3.890	3.791
6	5.795	5.601	5.417	5.242	5.076	4.917	4.767	4.623	4.486	4.355
7	6.728	6.472	6.230	6.002	5.786	5.582	5.389	5.206	5.033	4.868
8	7.652	7.325	7.020	6.733	6.463	6.210	5.971	5.747	5.535	5.335
9	8.566	8.162	7.786	7.435	7.108	6.802	6.515	6.247	5.985	5.759
10	9.471	8.983	8.530	8.111	7.722	7.360	7.024	6.710	6.418	6.145
Year	**11%**	**12%**	**13%**	**14%**	**15%**	**16%**	**17%**	**18%**	**19%**	**20%**
1	0.901	0.893	0.885	0.877	0.870	0.862	0.855	0.847	0.840	0.833
2	1.713	1.690	1.668	1.647	1.626	1.605	1.585	1.566	1.547	1.528
3	2.444	2.402	2.361	2.322	2.283	2.246	2.210	2.174	2.140	2.106
4	3.102	3.037	2.974	2.914	2.855	2.798	2.743	2.690	2.639	2.589
5	3.696	3.605	3.517	3.433	3.352	3.274	3.199	3.127	3.058	2.991
6	4.231	4.111	3.998	3.889	3.784	3.685	3.589	3.498	3.410	3.326
7	4.712	4.564	4.423	4.288	4.160	4.039	3.922	3.812	3.706	3.605
8	5.146	4.968	4.799	4.639	4.486	4.344	4.207	4.078	3.954	3.837
9	5.537	5.328	5.132	4.947	4.772	4.607	4.451	4.303	4.163	4.031
10	5.889	5.650	5.426	5.216	5.019	4.833	4.659	4.494	4.339	4.193

Notes

Chapter 1

1. Shakespeare, W. *The tempest* (1611), act 4, scene 1.

2. A trust is an entity commonly used in estate planning. For more detailed information have a look at Pareto, C. (2010). *Pick the perfect trust.* Retrieved from http://www.investopedia.com/articles/pf/08/trust-basics.asp

Chapter 2

1. Most readers will know this as a *balance sheet.* This is an accounting name that doesn't really suit what the statement tries to explain. "Resources statement" is the term I have chosen to use throughout this book because I believe it puts in plain words what this statement should be all about.

2. Porter, M. E. (1980). *Competitive strategy.* New York, NY: The Free Press.

Chapter 5

1. *U.S. government bonds, treasury & municipal bond yields.* Retrieved November 20, 2010, from Bloomberg: http://www.bloomberg.com/markets/rates-bonds/government-bonds/us/

2. *Where are we with market valuations?* Retrieved November 20, 2010, from Gurufocus.com: http://www.gurufocus.com/stock-market-valuations.php

3. *Stock quote for CISCO Systems Inc.* Retrieved November 20, 2010, from MSN Money: http://www.moneycentral.msn.com/detail/stock_quote?symbol=CSCO&ww=1

Chapter 7

1. Hammer, M. (2003). *Agenda.* New York, NY: Three Rivers Press, p.101.

Chapter 10

1. Rein, S. (2009, June 16). *Why most M&A deals end up badly.* Forbes.com: http://www.forbes.com/2009/06/16/mergers-acquisitions-advice-leadership-ceonetwork-recession.html

Epilogue

1. U.S. secretary of defense (1961–1968) and his belief about what led to defeat in the Vietnam War.

2. I am grateful to Charles Handy for introducing me to this analogy, which first appeared in his book *The Age of Paradox* ([1994]. Boston, MA: Harvard Business School Press).

3. From a speech by Sir Winston Churchill at the Mansion House, London, on November 10, 1942.

Index

Note: The *f* following page numbers refers to figures.

OTHER TITLES IN OUR FINANCIAL ACCOUNTING COLLECTION

Series Editor: **Ken Ferris**

An Executive's Guide for Moving From U.S. GAAP to IFRS by Peter Walton

CPSIA information can be obtained at www.ICGtesting.com
261684BV00002B/3/P

9 781606 492338